Little e, Big Commerce

How to Make a Profit Online

Timothy Cumming

To Shirley, Holly and Ruby

First published in Great Britain in 2001 by
Virgin Publishing Ltd
Thames Wharf Studios
Rainville Road
London
W6 9HA

A catalogue record for this book is available from the British Library.

ISBN 0 7535 0542 8

Series Consultant: Professor David Storey
Joint Series Editors: Robert Craven, Grier Palmer

Series design by Janice Mather at Ben Cracknell Studios
Typeset by Phoenix Photosetting, Chatham, Kent
Printed and bound in Great Britain by Mackays of Chatham PLC

Contents

Acknowledgements

'Fear the clock' were the first thoughts that entered my mind after Virgin asked me to write this book. 'How can I write a book and run my e-Commerce agency at the same time?'

And 'fear the clock' is pretty good advice for any entrepreneur reading this book. In the five months that it took to write and edit this work, the world of e-Commerce of course moved forward dramatically. 'Of course', because we've all become familiar with the speed at which the Internet develops. So how is it that none of us ever seem to get familiar with developing our businesses at the same speed? I suppose that in many senses that was the starting point for this book – just how can the entrepreneur keep up?

Today, we worry about web technology in a way that we never worried about the phone or the fax machine. E-commerce seems to have brought with it not just its own baggage, but its own luggage rack, too! Senior managers must make decisions for which they seem inadequately qualified. Entire technology departments are formed overnight. Venture capitalists throw millions of pounds at very inexperienced business people. Companies build sites because they feel compelled to keep up, not because they want to grow their business. And all because of the Internet.

Overcoming this madness was my main goal in writing this book. I hope I have simplified the choices, and reduced the risks of entrepreneurship in e-Commerce.

A big thank-you to Robert Craven, Jim McLaughlin and Chris Hawcroft for being bigger sources of inspiration than they know. To David Siegel, Evan Schwartz, Richard Wilson and Colin Gilligan for their provocative writing. And to Sally Wilton, Bob Morgan and Don Lunn for wittingly or unwittingly sending me on the best journeys of my life.

A big thank-you also to the excellent *Internet Works* magazine for its consistent and insightful writing and research, to which I turned when no other books or publications were available.

A special word of gratitude to Caroline and Michael Berkeley and to Elizabeth Elston, who so kindly provided their peaceful, isolated country homes (your computers should be working OK now), and to Rowhill Grange in Dartford who so expensively provided their health-and-fitness facilities when my brain became addled.

Many thanks also to my team at hello-business.com, especially Charlotte Lambert, who saw me through thick and thin in the writing period, and who contributed good feedback on all the ideas. Thanks also to Andy Kinloch for his deep knowledge and calm approach.

And, last but not least, my biggest thanks go to my wider family for encouragement and to my immediate family, who tolerated an absent father on many weekday evenings and weekends, and who provided friendly support when I needed it most.

Foreword
by Sir Richard Branson

It feels a bit odd to be writing a foreword to a business book. Perhaps it's because I haven't always done business by the book myself. Sometimes I've regretted that, and sometimes I've been glad that I followed my instincts instead of doing what conventional advisers might have recommended.

One thing I've learned is that there's no right way to do things in life. There is no 'magic bullet' for success in business. What works for Virgin Atlantic might not be right for British Airways; what suits your business could be completely wrong for someone else's. But any advice that can help you beat the odds and succeed in business has got to be a good thing. Listening to lots of people's ideas before taking a decision has always been something I have strongly believed in.

Every book in this series has been written by an expert in his or her field, and they've come up with lots of interesting and thought-provoking ideas. But the most important thing is to do what you personally feel is right.

Business should be fun. Enjoy what you do, and success comes within reach.

Good luck!

This excellent book is about profit and productivity on the Internet. Such a book would have been unthinkable even one or two years ago. When e-Commerce burst like a meteor upon many of us, it seemed that websites would somehow automatically generate business. We have learned that this is not so.

Making a healthy profit – online or offline – is about being productive and professional. But in the online world, things are different. As Timothy Cumming emphasises in this book, 'e-Commerce doesn't change everything, but it does change a lot'.

So exactly what does it change and what remains unchanged?

The big changes are that the customer is ever more in the driving seat. Competition is more fierce. Change is quicker. Innovation is rewarded more. For the smaller enterprise, perhaps a more playful approach to business is required. Indeed, e-Commerce has brought the average age of the entrepreneur crashing down. Those e-Commerce businesses with the highest public profile – defined as those where supposedly canny financial institutions are most prepared to lavish funds – seem to be run by a bunch of kids. Yet our research at Warwick only a few years ago told us that businesses established by young people were perhaps two and a half times more likely to fail than those established by individuals in late middle age. Bankers in the past, for good reason, had tended to shy away from providing funding for the young entrepreneur. Yet today, pretty much the same financial institutions exhibit an almost Klondike mentality in rushing to provide financial support for new e-Commerce businesses.

All this might lead you to believe the world has turned upside down – the so-called Paradigm Shift. But, bankers are certainly not stupid. They have grasped, perhaps more quickly than most, that the world has changed in some respects, but not in others.

Reading Cumming's book also makes clear this continuity. For example, his advice on developing a successful e-Commerce enterprise centres confidently on the fundamentals of running any highly successful business. We know from our work on 'Ten Percenters' (research for Deloitte & Touche into the most successful 10 per cent of UK businesses) that the key to success for medium-sized UK companies is their ability to identify and satisfy niche groups of customers. Of course it is helpful if these businesses are well-managed, but what distinguishes the sheep from the goats is the identification of the niche and its exploitation. In other words, proven and familiar marketing techniques apply online too!

In my view, what e-Commerce has done, in a genuinely revolutionary way, is to create niches on an unprecedented scale over short periods of time. What Cumming shows is that these niches need to be understood and exploited competitively, innovatively, productively and at speed.

He usefully introduces the idea of speed segmentation, distinguishing between the low-speed and the high-speed customer. He encourages the business owner to consider which category is dominant amongst their customer group and to then deliver a service that is appropriate for either or both groups. He explains innovation and value in clear, jargon-free terms.

The speed with which information disseminates on the net means, as Cumming demonstrates, that e-customers always have the upper hand. But the business has to make this work to its advantage. There is every reason to believe the good news will circulate every bit as fast as the bad. Cumming importantly reiterates that the satisfied customer is the single most powerful marketing tool available. In e-Commerce it is critical to differentiate yourself from the competition. Equally critical is to know and understand that competition, and here the book contains a delightful passage on 'how to spy on your competitors'.

If profit and productivity are the underlying themes of this book, then my message to the reader is absorb and apply this excellent guide to digital commerce. Profit and productivity will surely follow.

Professor David Storey
Director, Centre for Small and Medium Sized Enterprises
Warwick Business School, University of Warwick

WHAT IS e-COMMERCE?

What exactly is e-Commerce and how does it work?

What it is and what it isn't

e-Commerce is selling, transacting or providing goods and services on the Internet. It's little e, big commerce, because if you're in business the commerce matters much more than the e!

And, if you don't read any further in this book than here, then at least you'll have gained an insight that many online companies overlook. The majority of online businesses fail. Why? It's usually because there's insufficient awareness – and action – in these critical elements of the business:

- Commercial management
- Real, not claimed, value
- True understanding of the customer's needs
- Rock-solid business model
- Suitable online elements added to the product or service
- Imaginative and relevant business targets
- Understanding the correct level of investment
- Appropriate use of the Internet for promotion
- Fast defensive capability against competitor action
- Strong innovation programme

When small or new Internet businesses combine these elements, they become strong and capable of defending themselves against even the largest and most powerful competitors.

And you can follow their path by putting these elements into your e-Commerce programme before you start. You're going to be able to arm yourself with the experience of others. So let the commerce lead and the technology follow!

Technology is the means, value is the end

Recently, two entrepreneurs asked my agency to help them start up their Internet business. Their idea was big. They were going to change the utilities market for the little guys – for small businesses and for consumers. Their idea was quite simple: create a shop where customers could compare water, power and telecom packages and then buy the one that best suited their needs (if you've ever tried to compare these kinds of packages you'll know how hard this is!). Great idea. And originally the two entrepreneurs had drafted a phenomenal list of functions and buttons that would appear on the website. But, after just a few days of thinking and planning, together we came to realise that the principal driver behind the success of this site was going to be a combination of personal service and comprehensive supplier knowledge. The website was merely to be a means of delivering that service. This may well be the case with your business, too.

A business is not viable merely because it trades on the Internet. The net is a medium, nothing more, nothing less – like the phone or the radio – so let's not get dazzled by its special features. Why, then, does every daily newspaper contain a business section on the net? Why does every billboard advert and every TV commercial carry a web address? Why do the European and American technology stock listings Easdaq and Nasdaq even exist? Still today, senior business figures, political leaders and many entrepreneurs focus on the 'e' – the medium. Because it's growing fast. It's visible. It's different from other media. But more important, much more important than the 'e', is the 'Commerce'.

The days of the overvalued dotcom companies are largely gone. Good thing, too. The inflated price of technology-based companies in the stock market has been responsible for gold-rush fever. But seven in ten Internet start-ups fail. That's better than the Klondike's nine in ten! Of course, we read only about the success stories. Nobody brags about his or her incompetence. Yet many entrepreneurs (and many non-entrepreneurs!) in the last few years have run before they could walk; rushed at initial flotation before they could genuinely offer investor value; thrown good money after bad; started sites that have failed badly.

Happily, we have reached a first-stage maturity in net software, and technology is no longer the battleground – value is. Value is king now. And how familiar that feels! We spent the last two decades in business driving up value – cutting costs, innovating, marketing, building quality and listening to customers. Your business probably participated in these development programmes. So you're probably comfortable with value already. That's a nice starting point, isn't it?

The mantra from the late nineties' net gurus was 'digitise or die'. Microsoft proudly proclaimed, 'If you're not online you're lunch'. The informed forecast was hyperbolic growth of e-Commerce and the resulting extinction of the offline business. That means your business! Hmm. You're still here? You're still trading? Sure, maybe you could do better – grow faster, trade more profitably – but you're hardly bankrupt, are you? Even if you have an e-Commerce site, your business is probably largely offline even now. Lunched on or even outperformed by superdigital net-only businesses? Doubt it. So where did the forecast screw up?

The netheads focused on technology. It's worth pointing out that many of them were technology suppliers themselves and so had a vested interest in your believing their shrieks. To focus on technology is to focus on the means, not the ends, of business. And other means include telephone, newspapers, TV, radio and direct mail. When these media were first adopted by businesses, the in-media experts also forecast a revolution in business methods. 'Running a radio campaign is like turning a sales tap on,' said many (delighted) first-time advertisers, some of whom I served when I worked in commercial radio.

But did a new breed of postapocalyptic business survivors emerge? Hardly. More like normal companies with new telesales teams, to deal with the spikes in demand caused by national advertising. Sure, they traded a little differently. Their strategies altered. And eventually their methods and structures changed as the volume of their new-media sales rose. But this was evolution. Not revolution. And, without doubt, the ends topped out over the means as the key drivers of these changes.

Today, as ever, the end in any business transaction is value. And value starts with the customer. So if we're all so good at developing value, and if we're talking evolution, not revolution, why isn't e-Commerce a walk in the park? Has something happened to the customer? Absolutely.

e-Commerce starts with the e-customer

The customer – whether a consumer or a business – now wears two hats. The physical-world hat and the online hat. In the physical world, the customer uses social or written skills to choose and buy. In the online world, the customer uses technology skills to buy. What implications drop out of this seemingly innocuous difference?

Online world

'I hate you contacting me'
'You've got my attention for seven seconds'

'I don't believe your sales waffle'
'I want to speak to your customers more than you'
'I won't buy unless it's easy'
'I don't trust you with my credit card'

Physical world

'I'll wait a minute or two'
'Thank you'
'I'll pay now'
'Thanks for your help'

It's hard to believe it's the same person when one hat comes off and the other goes on. This schizophrenic collection of attitudes describes your online customer – because your online customer is offline too. So how do we understand and categorise this new e-customer?

We segment. Segmentation is the business of dividing your market into segments. Each segment should have unique characteristics that require to be serviced in different ways. Why bother with segmentation? Well, for one thing, it helps you to target your services and products more accurately at specific groups of users. But the main advantage of segmentation is focus. Focusing your benefits. Focusing your products. Focusing your marketing messages. Focusing your prices. Focusing your new-product development. And, above all, focusing your customer-retention efforts.

When you become that focused, your competitive advantage has grown. Now you're ready to compete with the best. You've become more responsive. And that means that your business is now much more suited to the Internet and to e-Commerce.

So what basis do we use for segmenting Internet customers?

Segmenting by communication

Some e-customers want to learn all about you, your uniqueness and your success stories. They're prepared to learn.

And some e-customers want to share ideas or comments with you and your other customers. They're prepared to teach.

When we combine these differing and defining aspects, we get a simple list of four stereotypes.

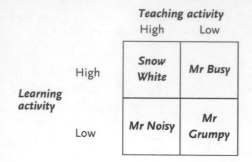

Now these kinds of customers were around before the Internet. But the technologies that they used didn't support the very personal and very public business of teaching or learning. The Internet has merely permitted them to act in a natural way and release something inside them that was always there.

When we look at teachers and learners, we notice four familiar kinds of individual. Perhaps you have customers just like them right now. Each stereotype needs to be treated differently. Let's take a closer look at their behaviour, what defines them and how to treat them.

- **Snow White**

  The perfect customer – she reads your site, follows your arguments, communicates with you and shares her enthusiasm for you with other customers on your discussion groups. You can send her unsolicited emails and ask her for her view or feedback on almost any aspect of your business – she'll be honest and helpful. She's rare – maybe less than 1 per cent of your customer base or visitor community will be Snow Whites.

- **Mr Noisy**

  A useful, vocal customer who will express his views with you and your other customers. He might be a little self-opinionated, and will have a tendency towards not reading or using your site fully. But, as a rule, these individuals will give you a broader picture of possible customer needs. They may buy less or buy less frequently. Again, Mr Noisy is rare, perhaps 5 per cent of your audience.

- **Mr Busy**

  This customer doesn't sound off much, and is possibly more passive than the others, although he is likely to be a frequent purchaser or visitor. But he does understand and use your site effectively for his own ends. He's prepared to learn about you and your products and services, and will probably read your emails. This is almost the ideal customer – tolerant, open and engaged. Perhaps 10 per cent of your customers are Mr Busy.

- **Mr Grumpy**
  Don't provoke these customers! Don't expect anything from them except sales. They speak with their credit cards. They have little or no respect for your company. They may like your website and the convenience it provides – but they'll never let you know. And, no surprises, Mr Grumpy comprises the vast majority of your audience – perhaps as high as 80–85 per cent!

By the way, my percentage figures here are loose and are not the result of research – they're just rounded figures from my own experience.

Segmenting by familiarity

Another way to segment your customers is by their familiarity with your site. Every visitor to your site has a familiarity level, which can be defined as beginner, intermediate or advanced. Beginners may not be technically proficient, but they have the same ability to learn as advanced users. It's helpful to treat each different familiarity level in an appropriate way, and of course with respect.

- **The beginner**
  The beginner usually teaches herself by simply trying things. She'll click buttons and links just to see what happens. Because she has less experience than the other users, she won't be looking in the usual places for navigation or content. She won't know to click on your logo to get home. She won't know instinctively how to use your search feature. She won't expect contact details to be in the 'About us' area. So you have to help her. You have to make sure that every feature and every button works as intuitively as possible. Your greatest concern with the beginner is making sure that she can get straight to the information that she needs. This is largely about getting navigation and design working effectively, but it's also about keeping content simple.

  Generally, she won't stay around long. She will give you only a short amount of her time before she becomes bored or gives up. And don't forget: these are the customers you fought hardest to win. These first-time visitors were the most expensive to get on to the site. So treat them with respect and make sure your investment is not wasted.

- **The intermediate**
The intermediate has already visited your site. He has learned to navigate his way. He knows where the valuable content lies. He knows where his favourite bits are. He may even have bought something already from your site. He is now ready to make the relationship leap by registering his details into your database, or by joining your community and sharing his thoughts and ideas with other customers. So you need to encourage him. Help him to make his first product review. Make it easy for him to find customer ratings and feedback. Lead him towards engaging in conversation with other like-minded customers.

    The main aim with trying to manage the intermediate is to convert him to expert status. The intermediate has made a leap of faith, has jumped in both feet first, and now it's your turn to reward him. Not just with the information and products that he wants, but also with the relationship that he deserves. Make sure you have specialist discussion areas for the intermediate, and real customer service on the phone and on email to nourish the relationship.

- **The advanced**
The advanced user already belongs. She feels she has a place on your site and among your customer community. She has been using your discussion forums for some time. She has developed relationships with other customers. She has become, if you're lucky, an ambassador for your business. And, if you neglect to serve her, she will be spreading the bad word about your business and your service.

    The trick with advanced users is to recognise that you cannot control them. They should control you. After all, they are customers with whom you have developed a strong relationship and who have come to trust you. Their experience, their needs, their attitudes towards you should be driving both your communications programme and your product-development programme. Working closely with advanced users is one of the first steps towards making your company truly customer-centred.

Segmenting by demographics

Probably the most obvious method of grouping your customers into useful stereotypes is by conventional means. If you're a good entrepreneur, you'll already be doing this. Here are some common examples:

Business segmentation examples

- Company turnover (e.g. <£1m, £1–£5m, £5m+)
- Business activity (e.g. chemist, supermarket, newsagent)
- Location (e.g. M25, three-mile radius, Scotland)
- Employee numbers (e.g. under 25, over 500)
- Channel (members of Institute of Directors, visitor to FT site)

Here's an example of business segmentation in action at www.dell.com:

a) Domestic
b) Small office, home office (SoHo)
c) Small business (under 25 staff)
d) Medium business (25–500 staff)
e) Large business (over 500 staff)
f) Educational
g) Not for profit

For each of these segments Dell has bundled differing prices, differing products, differing features and differing levels of customer support and service. It has also tailored the visual environment – the look and feel – of the site for each different segment. It has in effect created different zones of the site for different market segments. This allows Dell to focus very closely on maximising the profits and the customer retention of these different groups – and of course the specific needs of these individual customers.

Consumer segmentation examples

- Age (e.g. teens, under-25s over-25s)
- Sex/sexual identity (e.g. male, female, gay, lesbian)
- Occasion (e.g. weekly shopper, occasional, special trip)
- Family (no kids, young family, teenage family, empty nest)

Here's an example of consumer segmentation in family travel:

a) Sporty Family is focused on water, competitive and leisure-based sports, and tends to seek facilities-based resorts
b) Learning Family seeks cultural, historical and educational locations and is likely to put up with unusual accommodation and transport in the name of the authentic experience
c) Regular Family usually seeks sun and beach, is generally undemanding in outlook and is likely to buy a package holiday

d) Adventurous Family is looking for challenges and possibly danger – such as rock climbing, sailing and trekking; it is likely to prefer good weather locations but this is by no means a requirement

e) Varied Family seeks a mix-and-match approach: for example, a sporty beach holiday or a historic tour near the sea

f) Undecided Family may have no clear-cut view of what it wants until a suggestion rings true

Segmenting by speed

One of the demands that I hear most frequently in my work is for speed. 'It's got to be faster than a search engine', 'it's got to be really really simple and really fast to load'. While there's always something we can do to make the site as lean and small – and therefore fast to load – as possible, speed is largely defined by the end user's connection and the site payload (the total volume of data transfer). During the late 1990s, there was a strong tendency towards designing for the lowest common denominator – in other words, towards creating the minimum payload. This meant keeping graphics and picture components to a minimum, and to a large extent reducing the design standards to a minimalist approach.

Today, it's still important to accommodate the user with the lowest connection speed. But there's a growing community of customers with medium- and high-speed Internet connections. Many of them have developed a taste for the visually rich, for lush graphics. It's not wise to ignore them, or their expectations of highly graphical sites. Now, as broadband services start to make an impression on the UK and European marketplace, both businesses and consumers are significantly increasing their viewing capabilities.

So which is better? Should we focus on the low-speed customer or the high-speed customer? The answer is both. It's a balance. Your site should serve both communities. And, not surprisingly, the cost in terms of time and money of creating that balance has gone up considerably. The choice now is: either develop five or six versions of the same site for different browsers and different access speeds, or pay a price in terms of lower customer retention as visitors migrate from your site to more glamorous-looking or visually acceptable sites.

The consequence of this is clear. Increase your budget, employ your own web team or reposition your site as a no-frills enterprise.

Access speed

		High	Low
Browser version	High	**Big Dynamic**	**Lean Dynamic**
	Low	**Big Antique**	**Lean Antique**

As you can see from this matrix, the impact of speed and browser technology is mainly on design. If your customers fall into these four categories (and most audiences do) then you need four sites, or at least four variants of one site.

In Chapter 5, we'll get into how to work with these differing segments.

B2B, B2C, B2P and B2A

Every business is different. And every channel – or route to market – is different. Taking the right approach to e-marketing starts with knowing what these channels are.

Selling glassware to consumers on the net is clearly very different from selling dentistry. Yet they're both B2C (business-to-consumer). And the same starting points for e-marketing may well apply.

Both businesses must reach a wide variety of customers. Pulling first-time visitors on to the site will be a challenging, and predominantly paper-based, activity. Customers are likely to be happy using credit cards for payment. Neither business has a huge marketing budget. Both businesses must carefully manage their ability to deliver within a time frame that's acceptable to the customer.

Reaching the consumer is the key to the success of these businesses. If they were providing services to the business community, their approach might be entirely different. So let's have a look at the four main channels that are open to Internet marketers.

Business-to-business (B2B)

Most industry specialists forecast B2B to become the highest sales and growth area on the Internet by 2002. If your business is B2B, your main goal will be delivering business services or products to other businesses.

Some common online and offline components in B2B are:

- Credit accounts, not credit-card sales
- Telesales and direct-mail support
- Internet affiliates
- Client support staff
- Client retention or loyalty programmes
- PR and trade-press advertising

Business-to-consumer (B2C)

B2C is what got e-Commerce going. Simple credit-card sales were the basis of success for the giants of e-Commerce such as Amazon.com and EasyJet.co.uk. Some of the frequent online and offline components that are used in B2C are:

- Credit-card sales
- Online support by email
- Affiliate programmes
- One- to three-day delivery
- Television, bill-board and other conventional advertising

Business-to-portal (B2P)

B2P is the new kid on the block. The game here is promoting your business to a portal site (a 'gateway' site which connects buyers and suppliers together in one marketplace). Generally, with B2P, you keep your own branding and sell through the portal. In this emerging form of marketing, the following online and offline components seem to prevail:

- A brief contract with the portal
- Royalty or commission-based programme with the portal
- Portal-specific promotions

Check out SharePeople.co.uk to see how Reuters' share information has been completely re-packaged by SharePeople (and paid for!).

Business-to-affiliate (B2A)

B2A is also quite new. The aim here is to charge your affiliate for your services by providing them with a 'white label' website, which they over-brand with their own design and colour scheme. The effect is that your affiliate provides the same service on their site as you do on yours. Perhaps there are fewer established trends here, but many affiliate marketeers seem to go for:

- A brief contract with the affiliate
- A royalty- or commission-based programme with the affiliate
- A contra arrangement, whereby content may be exchanged from one site to the other
- An advertising or editorial contra arrangement

Take a look at Yahoo.com or Independent.co.uk and see if you can spot content provided by B2A marketers.

Which Internet pieces do what?

The Internet is made up of three main components: websites, email and discussion groups. Each has its own characteristics and its own set of strengths.

Websites are particularly good at demonstrating, educating and publishing. Email is best for informal one-to-one and one-to-many communication. Discussion groups are excellent at networking and sharing. So certain kinds of business activities are better suited to certain components of the Internet than others.

Website strengths

I sometimes think of websites as a cross between television, books and a librarian. Many of the characteristics of a website are found in these places.

Television demonstrates. It promotes. It shows the user not just pictures, but also how a product can actually be used. Similarly, websites can present positive messages and illustrate benefits. But they also permit the user to control how the product is demonstrated, and which parts of it are revealed and to what depth.

Books reveal information in depth. They follow a logical, sequential flow. They have a beginning, middle and end. Websites also carry information in depth. But they also offer the user control over that depth. They allow the user to read summaries, or dive straight down to deep-level copy, to skip around, to navigate easily to the parts of the information that they seek without having to follow the logical flow. So, although they provide depth, websites need to be constructed in such a way that they can be read in any order, with no logical flow.

Librarians act as your emissary. They have skills that you do not. They know exactly where to find the very thing that you seek. Librarians on websites are to be found in the search functions and the navigation system. Like librarians, they should be capable of helping you define your problem, as well as solving it.

So what are the consequences of this for your business? Here's a useful checklist to make sure that you're exploiting the main strengths of the web – your site should:

- ☐ Demonstrate your product or service
- ☐ Visually illustrate it, as well as textually describe it
- ☐ Demonstrate how your product or service is actually used by a customer
- ☐ Promote positively the benefits of using the product
- ☐ Clearly differentiate your product or service or the company itself from the competition

It's amazing how many companies absent-mindedly overlook these principal strengths. Make sure you check for the presence of all these components in your site's design and structure before you build it.

Email strengths

The principal strengths of email are directness and speed. Email can be used for very intimate one-to-one communication, or for broadcasting one-to-many messages. In the UK, many companies have adopted a formal style in their emails. This is in sharp contrast with the much briefer and generally more informal style adopted by many American companies. Most employees I know tend to react favourably to informal emails like this:

Hi Jerry.

Still keeping fit? We're opening a new gymnasium at our health club on the 15th next week. Top gear, nice Jacuzzi. Free champagne on the night!

Love to see you there – sports kit not required!

Keep well,

Jane
White Hat Health Club

By contrast, most people I know tend to glaze over when they receive emails like this:

Dear Jerry,

White Hat Health Club announces superb new gym facilities!

After two successful years, we are proud to announce the opening of our second gymnasium. Packed with all the latest equipment, the facilities offer fully insured, experienced and well-qualified practitioners across a variety of health-and-fitness programmes.

Put aside all your previous experiences and preconceptions of health clubs and fitness centres. We're a million miles away from any of them! Here are just a few of our services:

FOR THE ACTIVE GAL
Movement classes
Dance classes
Aromatherapy exercises
Body-active worker sessions
Weight-reduction programmes
Health screening
Chiropractic and sports therapy
Personal training

FOR THE ACTIVE GUY
Cardiovascular workout
Muscle-building programmes
Aerobic programmes
Weekend crash workout programmes
Personal fitness trainer

As a valued customer, you're cordially invited to attend our grand opening ceremony at 7 p.m. on 15 March. Please reply to this email if you wish to attend.

Best wishes,

J Parker
Customer Services Director
White Hat Health Club

Check out our website at www.whitehathealthclub.com for details of this month's special leg-waxing promotion!

This message may contain information that is legally privileged and/or confidential. If you are not the intended recipient, you are hereby notified that any unauthorised disclosure, copying, distribution or use of this information is strictly prohibited. Such notification notwithstanding, any comments or opinions expressed are those of the originator, not of White Hat Health Club or any of its subsidiary or parent (holding) organisations, unless otherwise explicitly stated.

Here, the message is formal in tone, too long, not tailored to Jerry, self-centred and not customer-focused, carries a women-only promotion, and shoots itself in the foot with a legal notice. Perhaps you might like to review your email policy when you think about the effect that poor use of email has on your audience.

Discussion group strengths

Perhaps the least understood of the three Internet pieces is the discussion group. This is an open area where people can share ideas or conduct two-way or multiple dialogues. Most web teams see it as a way of letting customers express their views, but can't see how to exploit it. Marketers like to think of them as the token nod towards the original ideals of the Internet – sharing, open, truthful and anti-marketing.

They're just like emails made public. This is not surprising, really, because they use the same technology. You send a message to the discussion group, which is effectively a public mailbox. Any member of the group can see the entire contents of the mailbox, and reply to any message. So each message may have a string of replies, replies to those replies and replies to those replies to previous replies and so on. These strings are called 'threads' in the web world. Here's the kind of pattern you often see:

CAR PAINT SCRATCHES
Anyone got any ideas on where to find car paint scratch filler?
Frank

RE: CAR PAINT SCRATCHES
Try www.gifford-paint.com – they've got some
Sheila

RE: RE: CAR PAINT SCRATCHES
I looked and couldn't see any
Gerry

RE: RE: CAR PAINT SCRATCHES
Found it at www.gifford-paints.com/shop/scratch. Thanks Sheila
Frank

If you're not a regular discussion group user, you may not be aware of the poor commercial exploitation of this area. Frequently, you'll find it hard to get what you want from a discussion group. They are generally very disappointing. But they needn't be. A good discussion group should enable you to:

☐ Know why you should join, and make it easy to do so

☐ Meet experts or like-minded individuals who like to help or collaborate

☐ Easily locate the topic you're interested in

☐ Predict what's likely to happen if you submit anything

☐ Show how the company acts on issues that arise from the discussion group

☐ Take action, based on your views or those of the community

So it's a good idea to build voting or rating functionality into the group, and obvious listening and responding devices. It's good to get your staff to join the discussion group and, where appropriate, contribute. It's good to structure the topics and provide a search facility that allows people to get to their topics as quickly as possible. It's good to write a help file, an 'aims' page that describes the purpose and possibly a charter that says what the rules are (such as 'no selling').

Perhaps when you build your site, you'd like to consider adding in an effective discussion group that's not merely a chat area, but which offers benefits to customers and allows them to take action.

How money is transferred

Broadly speaking, there are two different types of money online. The first is signed e-money (such as a cheque or a credit card) and the second is anonymous e-money (also known as digital cash). As an entrepreneur, you may have very different reasons for choosing which you prefer, but the best reasons of all are for the convenience of your customer.

Signed e-money reveals the identity of the payer. This allows companies, banks, authorisers and anyone involved in the payment chain to keep accountable records of who paid what to whom and when. Anonymous e-money on the other hand behaves very much like real cash. It's withdrawn from a wallet or an account, and is spent without trace, so no one can trace the source or sources.

There are two varieties of each type of e-money: online e-money and offline e-money.

Online means you need to interact with a bank (via modem or network) to conduct a transaction with a third party. Offline means you can conduct a transaction without having to directly involve a bank.

So much for theory. While these payment methods are all true for the USA, their diversity is hardly found in Europe at all.

Credit card

Payment on the Internet is still dominated by credit cards. There's a good reason for this. They're familiar. They work. They come bundled with a large number of anti-fraud, anti-theft measures. And something we all tend to forget – credit. Most cards give you 45 days or thereabouts.

When your customer pays by credit card, she's really kicking off the following chain of events:

1 The customer's click submits full payment details to you and issues an instruction to proceed
2 Your software hands the details to your authorisation service, which checks that the credit card is legal, valid and liquid
3 Your software or your authorisation service (your choice) then issues a notice to your bank to move the money
4 The bank moves the money

It's really that simple. Of course, you have to pay two organisations here. The authorisation company (such as WorldPay or NetBanx) and your bank. And you have to have a merchant service set up with your bank – an account that permits you to take credit-card payments. They both usually have set-up fees and commissions, which diminish as your sales increase. You can pay a total of 4 per cent to 8 per cent to these people depending on how much you sell online.

There are other payment methods, much trumpeted by their inventors and those who offer the service. There are digital cash and digital cheques, digital credits and micropayments. To date, the one thing these methods tend to have in common is their low availability. Which is a bit sad, really, because they're all very good ideas. However, many online customers (even in the USA) are unfamiliar with them and are sometimes a little baffled by requests to download plug-ins or digital features when they just want to buy something quickly. And, of course, just about everyone has a credit card.

Digital cash

It's likely that digital cash will make a good entry to the European market in 2001, so I've explained it here. To accept digital cash, you must have the digital equivalent of a cash register. You can get one from companies such as eCash. When your customer wants to pay you this is what happens:

1 The customer's click submits full payment details to you and issues an instruction to withdraw cash from their digital wallet
2 Your digital cash register retrieves the money and leaves a payment reference or receipt in your customer's wallet

3 Your customer can refill their wallet by moving money from an online bank or by credit card into the digital wallet

4 You empty the digital cash from your cash register into your online bank account using the bank's website

Here's an extract from the eCash website, which explains how you pay for goods with digital cash:

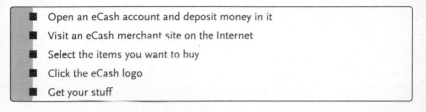

- Open an eCash account and deposit money in it
- Visit an eCash merchant site on the Internet
- Select the items you want to buy
- Click the eCash logo
- Get your stuff

So, if you want to sell goods to customers with digital cash, you need to become a merchant of a digital-cash company such as eCash. To find out how to do this, conduct a search on any major engine for 'digital cash' and 'UK' for the latest suppliers of this service. Each provider has a description of how to become a merchant on their site.

There are other methods of online payment, which have appeared in the USA, such as Digital Cheques and micropayments.

Not surprisingly, the payment and e-money field changes on a monthly basis. With every bank and financial entrepreneur rushing to get a piece of every customer's action and every supplier's transaction, it's best to turn to the Internet itself for the latest information on products and prices. Here's a list of useful resources for the latest information on payment methods. It includes digital cash, cheques and micropayment:

- www.authorizenet.com – Authorizenet processes credit card and checking account transactions.
- http://mkn.co.uk/bank – BankNet offer an electronic cheque system in sterling. In the future it will also incorporate the SET protocols.
- www.checkfree.com – CashBox, from Intertrader, is a payment management system that supports Internet loading and spending of a variety of Internet payment types including Mondex.
- www.1clickcharge.com – 1ClickCharge is an account-based micropayment scheme for the web, allowing charges to be made with a single click.
- www.clickshare.com/clickshare – Clickshare is a publishing system to track movements and settle charges for digital transactions.
- www.creditnet.com – Credit Card Network have a credit-card authorization system using SSL.

- www.articweb.com – CurrencyOne from ArticWeb is a credit-card solution. It is used in Bank of Ireland's Clikpay credit-card payment system. ArticWeb also have a voice-authenticated payment system.

- www.cybank.net – Cybank is a web payment system whereby purchases are charged against funds held in a Cybank account.

- www.cybergold.com – Cybergold allows you to earn, and spend, money online.

- www.cybermoola.com – Cybermoola is a prepaid account system, which can be funded with prepaid cards or a credit card.

- www.cybersource.com – CyberSource offer real-time credit-card processing and other electronic-commerce services.

- www.datacash.com – DataCash, based in the UK, provide secure credit-card authorisation over SSL.

- www.awa.com/Ecash is a fully anonymous electronic cash system, using Chaum's blind signatures. Originally from DigiCash (until November 1998), acquired by eCash Technologies in August 1999.

- www.echarge.com/E-coin is a token-based micropayment system, which uses a client-wallet plug-in. Free tokens are currently available.

- www.efunds.com – Electronic Funds Clearinghouse provide payment transmission and intake conduits over the Internet.

- www.fundamo.com – Fundamo is an account-based mobile commerce architecture which allows mobile users to make and receive payments.

- www.globeid.com – Globe ID credit- and debit-card-based payment systems.

- www.ibill.com/ – iBill provides credit-card and cheque processing.

- www.i-escrow.com/ – i-Escrow is a third party which holds a buyer's money in trust until a vendor delivers purchased goods.

- www.zurich.ibm.com/Technology/Security/extern/ecommerce/ iKP.html – iKP: a family of secure-payment protocols from IBM.

- www.intercoin.com – InterCoin is an online billing service, with a try-before-you-buy attitude.

- www.itransact.com – iTransact provide credit-card, cheque and EFT payment processing.

- www.magex.com – Magex, backed by NatWest Bank, is an account-based payment system for encrypted content.

- www.mojonation.net – Mojo Nation uses accounts and micropayments to allow payment for use and provision of unused online resources. Reputations are used as a means of preventing double spending.

- www.mondex.com – Mondex smart-card-based payment scheme.

- www.mon-e.com – Mon-e is an account-based system that is funded using a real-world prepaid card.
- www.onlinecheck.com – Online Check Systems allows cheques to be accepted online.
- www.paylinx.com – Paylinx provide payment servers for credit-card processing.
- www.paypal.com – PayPal allows user-to-user payments, whereby the payer uses a credit card to pay money into another user's account.
- www.innovonics.com/pcpay/pcpayhome.html – PC Pay is a smart-card-based system for Internet payments and banking.
- www.propay.com – Propay.com is a person-to-person, account-based payment that also allows credit-card payments to be accepted by users.
- www.protonworld.com – Proton is a stored-value smart-card scheme (e-purse), originally issued in Belgium as an alternative to physical cash. It is now being adapted for Internet payments.
- www.qpass.com – QPass aggregates small purchases at multiple merchants and charges against a credit card periodically.
- www.secure-bank.com – Secure-Bank.Com provides online transaction-processing solutions for credit cards and cheque drafts, based on SSL.
- www.cyota.com – SecureClick, from Cyota, uses a one-time transaction number which is linked to a credit-card account, and is cleared through the credit-card network as normal by a merchant.
- www.mastercard.com/set – Secure Electronic Transaction (SET) from Visa/Mastercard.
- www.valley-Internet.com/securetrans – SecureTrans is a real-time credit-card processing system and electronic cheque service, using SSL.
- www.smartaxis.com – SmartAxis allows stored value held on smart cards to be used over the Internet. Currently Proton and Mondex cards are supported.
- www.surefirecommerce.com – SureFire Commerce provide credit-card transaction-processing services as part of their e-Commerce solutions.
- www.virtualpay.com – VirtualPay is an on-line bill-payment system.
- www.anacom.com/payment.htm – WebCharge, from Anacom, offers real-time credit-card processing services based on SSL.
- www.trivnet.com – WiSP, from Trivnet, is a payment system that uses the existing relationship with an ISP to allow third-party purchases to be billed by that ISP.
- www.worldpay.com – WorldPay provide multicurrency credit/debit-card and account-based micropayment solutions.

- http://x.com – X.com provides user-to-user payments based on a current account.
- http://paydirect.yahoo.com – Yahoo! PayDirect will allow user-to-user payments, provided by DotBank.com.
- www.portsoft.com – Ziplock is a credit-card payment system by which customers receive a key code to unlock the product only after it has been downloaded and their credit card authorised.

(I downloaded the original of this list from a source on the Internet that I can no longer find. If it's your list, please do email me at tim@hello-business.com – I'd just like to say thanks!)

Whichever payment system you choose, be sure that your customers can – and want to – pay that way.

How goods are delivered

Downloadable goods or services

If your product or service can be downloaded – say it's software, pictures or valuable data – then you clearly have no timing or dispatch issues. A master copy of your documents merely sits on your website, and is copied by the computer every time a customer downloads it.

But of course you'll have help-desk issues – customers need to ask questions when they've had no personal guidance on how to use the product. So for downloadable products I always think of delivery as availability of support. And the key issues here are:

☐ Good availability of help-desk staff
☐ Good training and recruitment of staff
☐ Sufficient phone lines
☐ Good stats on computer logging of calls
☐ Fast and human (not automated) email response times

Physical goods

Tangible boxed goods are a different matter. The key here is speed. Customers don't like to wait more than two days for delivery, and usually expect a courier to do the leg work. The nice part is that they're usually prepared to pay for this delivery speed. The nasty part is that free delivery is starting to become a competitive tool, especially in the £50–£150 purchase range.

Let's say you run a glassware company, selling drinking glasses to distributors and retailers in the Midlands. Once you move online, you'll be able to sell to a national, if not international, market and sell direct to end users, not just distributors or retailers. So there are a number of big steps you'll have to take:

- ☐ Set up a merchant licence with your bank to handle credit-card sales
- ☐ Hook up the stock inventory system to the website so customers are warned if they order goods that cannot be delivered quickly
- ☐ Speed up dispatch to 48 hours
- ☐ Prepare for large orders from new (untrusted) customers – maybe protect yourself with payment insurance
- ☐ Handle small orders direct from the public – set up a small-orders dispatch team for 48-hour turnaround of these
- ☐ Calculate the extra cost of dispatch for small orders and increase retail prices to end users accordingly (small orders will be less productive)
- ☐ Set up a contract with a national courier or a specialist Internet fulfilment house, if you don't intend to deliver using your own staff

These steps may seem like common sense. They are. But it's astonishing how many companies think about these problems only *after* they've gone online, not before.

Must-have, show-stopping, drop-dead e-Commerce skills

When you move your business idea online, there are certain skills that will help you in everything you do. They'll also smooth the path for offline business. They are:

1 Listening skills
2 Learning skills
3 Creative skills
4 Adaptability skills
5 Truthfulness
6 Speed skills
7 Collaborative skills

No problem there, you may be thinking – we have those now.
Really? Put your hand on your heart and see if you comply with any of these:

☐ In the last three months, we have improved our product or service as a result of a customer suggestion

☐ We review what we have learned every month

☐ Our sales people listen 70 per cent and talk 30 per cent

☐ In the last six months, we've launched something genuinely unique to customers

☐ Our sales claims are 100 per cent honest and do not exaggerate

☐ In the last three months, we've changed our working methods

☐ In the last year, we've teamed up with one or more new affiliates or strategic partners

Still feeling good about your skills? The markers above indicate customer focus – the basis of successful e-Commerce. Now, many companies aspire to these kinds of claims, yet so few achieve them. They think that competition is about intensifying promotional effort – in other words, they think it's about pushing – when in fact it's the opposite. It's about pulling. About getting customers to demand – and get – value, improvement and honesty. And these are provided by a balance of responsive and creative skills. See the seven-point list at the beginning of this section.

The strange thing is that many entrepreneurs and managers are unaware that they – or their teams – already have these skills. In fact, I think this is the reason why the consultancy, incubator and e-Commerce industries are so successful: all we do is unlock something that's already there. Applying the right skills means applying the right actions, which means getting the right results.

Another plus here is that they're easier skills to use. Most people and most teams have them. For the moment, think about these skills. Think about how you might draw them out. An exercise I sometimes run with my clients is this:

1 Assemble your team; split them into four groups. Group 1 is the 'now' team and will act the way we do things now. Group 2 is the 'customer-focus' team and will act according to our new skills. Group 3 is the customer. Group 4 monitors and reports.

2 Get the customer to say what they want, in the way they normally say it.

3 Get the now team to respond, focusing on order taking, production or operations, delivery, customer service, pricing or discounting, quality, how you improve value, customer feedback, corrective action and internal communication.

4 Get the customer-focus team to respond in the same areas.

5 Get the monitoring team to identify the key differences.
6 Reassemble the whole group and discuss what changes will successfully bring about the customer-focus method.

For most companies conducting this exercise, they realise that the
skills issue is a red herring. They have the skills. They're just not using
them. And that's a management issue. And now you've just made a start
on improving management!

This exercise also applies to Internet start-ups, only slightly differently. Of course, you don't have a 'now' team, but the customer-focus
person can go through the same areas, and the monitoring person can
calculate the cost implications. This is usually an eye-opener for entrepreneurs who have conceived the perfect product for the perfect world,
and now have to create a real product for the real world.

What you'll need before going live

Besides the know-how, the people and the plan (to which we devote the
rest of this book), you will need a little technology. Often the first question my e-Commerce clients ask me is, 'What technology do we need?'
Let's have a look:

1 A website
2 Email
3 A security certificate
4 An online catalogue and shopping basket
5 A merchant agreement with your bank
6 Credit-card authorisation service from an Internet bank
7 Delivery mechanism to get your goods or services to customers

And where do you get all this? Unless you're seriously techie, don't
even think about it. An e-Commerce specialist will handle it all for you.
If you really do want to get involved with technology, have a look at the
final section of this book – and then dive in and buy a few three-inch-
thick computer manuals – good luck if you do!

So now we've covered the basics, let's turn our attention to your business. How does e-Commerce apply to you?

CHAPTER TWO

How does e-Commerce apply to my business?

How suited is my business to e-Commerce?

It's a deceptive question. The answer isn't always 100 per cent. Just about all businesses are suited to the Internet – those that can survive without a phone are about as many in number as those that can survive without email or a rudimentary brochure site. But e-Commerce is a different question altogether. It depends on a number of issues: what you do, how you work and your management team. Let's take a look at these three areas in practical terms.

Product/service suitability

Let's start with the product or service. Several components come into play here.

A) Download

First, the degree to which your product or service is downloadable. For instance, software, games and pictures, documentation or online publications, such as news or articles.

Often, service businesses believe that they cannot produce downloadable materials, because their core activity is essentially human. Actually, this is rarely the case. Professional-services firms can easily create simple ten-step guides, which educate their customers and at the same time promote the business. Business-services firms can produce reports, or even give away something free as a taster for their skills and expertise. Keynote has for many years published summary market information on its website as a high-value promotional taster for its chargeable services. Commonly, small businesses are reluctant to give away 'the family silver', fearful that competitors are watching the site closely. It is true that competitors may well lift ideas from your site. But a great many of the promotional benefits of being on the Internet lie in your ability to claim first-with-the-idea or market-leader status, no matter how small you are.

Also, boldly publishing valuable information conveys a clear message about how confident you are. And of course, it endears the customer.

The product:

- [ ] Is largely text, numbers or data in a database or
- [ ] Is largely electronic images or
- [ ] Is largely a computer file or a document or
- [ ] Is largely articles or news or
- [ ] Is a constantly changing kind of electronic feed or
- [ ] Is largely software itself or
- [ ] Is a hybrid of these or
- [ ] Requires PC-based software to work

So, what if you score high here? Congratulations, you're a natural e-business. But what if you score low? Consider which parts of your service or product could be made to be downloadable. Let's say that you publish paper magazines. You could easily put your leading feature articles online, either charging for or giving away free the download of these articles. A membership-based site may well be the best money-generating device in this case. Let's say that you run an HR or personnel consultancy. You could put many of your process documents and HR development tools online, again perhaps charging by membership model.

B) Catalogues

The second factor is the degree to which your product or service can be catalogued. If you have a range of services or products, each with different features, such as colour, size or type, then you may easily present your product portfolio as a catalogue. Most users are familiar with the visual concept and functionality of a catalogue and a shopping basket.

Your product:

- [ ] Has a variety of features such as colour, size, capacity, etc.
- [ ] Has a variety of optional extras such as metallic paint, insurance, dinner included
- [ ] Has clear pricing
- [ ] Has clear delivery dates

And your service:

- [ ] Has a variety of features such as duration, scale, resources
- [ ] Has clear-cut outcomes
- [ ] Clearly defines what's included and what's not

What if you score high here? You're lucky. You merely have to develop the right shopping basket and catalogue and you're in business. But what if you score low? Try to select parts of your service or product that can be shrink-wrapped. For a telecoms-installation business, this may be an audit, an upgrade to digital phones or the integration of voice and data circuits. For a transportation company, this may be a twelve-hour delivery, a twenty-four-hour delivery or a next-week delivery. In both cases it may well be that new services will have to be defined. It's often the case that businesses that have well-defined existing forms of services or products have to revisit them and make small or sometimes significant changes.

C) Delivery

The third factor is the ease with which your product or service can be delivered. If you manufacture physical products, or can process your service on your own premises, then your customers are likely to have a high degree of confidence in placing an order with you; they are less likely to worry about whether you can or cannot deliver.

Your product:

☐ Can be packed into a box
☐ Can be delivered by courier, van or lorry
☐ Is in stock or can be manufactured quickly

Your service:

☐ Can be conducted on your own premises or
☐ Can be conducted on your clients' premises on a bookable date or over a predictable period of time
☐ Has fixed or predictable outcomes
☐ Requires well-defined (the smaller the better) bursts of customer input

And if you score high here? You're well suited to fast e-Commerce. Of course, you'll need to develop reliable human delivery processes, but any business should be doing that. If you score low, try to create new ways of assuring your customer of delivery. Alternatively, you can create new services or products which can be delivered more easily. For instance, if you run an acupuncture centre, you could put your booking system online, or if you run a creative design agency, you could create new 3-day, 4-day and 5-day services, with artwork delivered over the Internet.

Business suitability

The way you work – or more importantly the way you aspire to work – also influences your suitability to e-Commerce. This involves customer service, day-to-day operations systems, supplier arrangements, customers and competitors.

Here's an illustration of a useful suitability tool, being used to rate two very different companies. 'What's the good in knowing?' you may be wondering. It helps you define your investment and your e-Commerce budget! If you score high, it's probably worth serious investment; if you score low, perhaps you should think twice about that bells-and-whistles site. Let's see how it works for two very different firms of solicitors who have contrasting suitability scores.

Example A
Practice: Lean Legals
Offering: Legal contracts without reinventing the wheel

Issue	Significance	Score	Weighted Score
Part of our product can be downloaded	5	10	50
Part of our product can be catalogued	2	3	6
Our product is easily delivered to the door	0	0	0
The net will not dilute our personal service	10	8	80
Growing % of customers are online	5	10	50
We have clear-cut work systems	10	9	90
Our competitors are trading online	10	5	50
Our management team is online	6	5	30
Our suppliers are online	0	0	0
Total	48	50	356
% Score			74.2%

Example B
Practice: Doggerel, Dust and Partners
Offering: Bespoke contracts only

Issue	Significance	Score	Weighted Score
Part of our product can be downloaded	2	10	20
Part of our product can be catalogued	2	0	0
Our product is easily delivered to the door	0	0	0
The net will not dilute our personal service	10	4	40

Example B – *continued*

Issue	Significance	Score	Weighted Score
Growing % of customers are online	5	10	50
We have clear-cut work systems	10	5	50
Our competitors are trading online	10	2	20
Our management team is online	6	0	0
Our suppliers are online	0	0	0
Total	45	31	180
% Score			40.0%

So some are more suited and others less so. It makes sense to invest accordingly. Perhaps Lean Legals should invest £20,000, and Doggerel & Dust only £10,000. This simple table can be a useful starting point for management.

Not everyone's business is suited to full-on e-Commerce. You should distinguish here between e-Commerce and online brochures (which do not transact). Unless you have a highly unusual business, or you provide a very localised service – such as a fish 'n' chip shop that caters for a few blocks – then it's hard to imagine a business that couldn't at least take orders or bookings online.

Management team suitability

The third major issue that comes into play with suitability is the management team itself. If your team isn't web-savvy, has a tendency towards production rather than customer focus, or is resistant to change, then you've got a problem!

What makes a management team suited to e-Commerce? In my experience, there isn't an absolute answer to this. I've known lumpy old-fashioned owner-managers become sparkling onliners, and I've seen very modern managers just blow their sites completely. But, in my view, some common characteristics do recur again and again in the management teams of successful e-Commerce companies:

- ☐ Customer focus, not production- or product-led thinking
- ☐ Flexibility and a welcoming attitude towards change
- ☐ Determination, especially when not succeeding
- ☐ Playfulness, mainly with ideas
- ☐ Candour and truthfulness, especially with analysis of performance
- ☐ Faith in more junior staff, especially when they are Internet 'eyes and ears'

☐ Speed in decision making
☐ Speed in controlling implementation

How far behind are we? It's a good question. Perhaps the most web-savvy individuals in your business have been banging the Internet drum for years. Perhaps you've only just come across the Internet as a serious business channel. It's easy to overlook this question and rush past it in your haste to get online quickly.

But if you can answer this question, you are halfway to defining the depth and breadth required for your new site. And monitoring the competition is the easiest way of marking how far behind you have slipped.

Competitor analysis

How do you gauge your competitors' sites, and thereby set a target for your own? Ask your customers or friends to rate each site on five or more areas – design, functionality, choice, product quality and price. Add your own extra areas if you wish, but remember: the more complex the model, the less differential you'll see between competitors and the more work you'll have to do.

If you're pushed for time, you can do this yourself, but beware of your prejudices! You need to be as impartial as possible!

Let's say you run a news-photography agency, selling news photos to media and direct to the public. To calculate the value of your competitors' combined websites and products, use the following formula:

$$\text{Design} \times \text{Functionality} \times \text{Choice} \times \text{Quality} \times \text{Price} = \text{Value}$$

You should score in marks out of ten, then calculate the averages for each area, and then index each company against the average. Sounds complicated? Look at this worked example (please note – a high price gets a low score):

Original Ratings

	Design	Functionality (incl payment)	Catalogue Choice	Product Quality	Price
Average	7.00	5.33	6.33	7.00	£32.16
Snaps	9	4	6	6	£30.00
NewPics	6	6	8	7	£28.50
PicHound	6	6	5	8	£37.99

Indexed Scores (setting average = 100%)

	Design	Functionality (incl payment)	Catalogue Choice	Product Quality	Price	Value
Average	100	100	100	100	100	100
Snaps	129%	75%	95%	86%	107%	84%
NewsPics	86%	113%	126%	100%	113%	137%
PicHound	86%	113%	79%	114%	85%	74%
You	**120%**	**120%**	**100%**	**100%**	**110%**	**158%**

So we can see from this example that, by setting our standards only a little higher than our competitors', we can go straight in at number one for value!

Most businesses find it tricky to evaluate competitors. This is probably only because they've never done it before, or they don't know where to start. Once you have an analytical framework in place, analysing competitors is a doddle.

I prefer to base competitor analysis on value. It's cleaner, simpler, and nine times out of ten it seems to hit the mark. You may choose to do it differently – for instance on the basis of delivery speed, service levels or innovation. If this works for you, and these aspects of competition in your marketplace are the most important, then use them!

Developing your site

Suppose you already have a website, and when you conduct your competitor analysis you reach the ugly conclusion that you score pretty low on the value stakes. How do you catch up?

Well, right away there are five areas in the competitor-analysis table where you could focus your improvement efforts. Assuming you've done your competitor analysis using customers to create the ratings, you may need to crawl inside their comments and their personal reactions before making changes to your site. Let's break down these five areas.

Design

Areas you might wish to consider include:

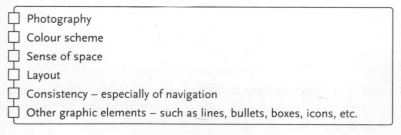

☐ Photography
☐ Colour scheme
☐ Sense of space
☐ Layout
☐ Consistency – especially of navigation
☐ Other graphic elements – such as lines, bullets, boxes, icons, etc.

Functionality

Areas you might wish to consider include:

- ☐ Catalogue
- ☐ Shopping basket
- ☐ Checkout and payment area
- ☐ Customer profiling
- ☐ Search functions
- ☐ Email this page to a friend
- ☐ Customisation – 'my space', 'my favourites', 'my homepage', etc.
- ☐ Quiz, competition, fun stuff, etc.

Catalogue choice

Areas you might wish to consider include:

- ☐ Number of products in catalogue
- ☐ Illustration of products
- ☐ Product descriptions and technical details
- ☐ Options for each product (e.g. colour, size, weight, etc.)
- ☐ Availability of products
- ☐ Delivery of products

Product quality

Obviously, this one goes to the heart of your business. Here are some high-level questions you might ask yourself:

- ☐ Does our product or service make at least 10 per cent difference to the customer?
- ☐ Is our product or service at least 10 per cent better than our competitors?
- ☐ Do over 10 per cent of our customers write or call to thank us?
- ☐ What are the benefits that our product or service produces?
- ☐ How can we increase the benefit by 10 per cent?

Price

Last but not least, consider making changes to your prices. But before you do so beware! You should really create a spreadsheet revenue model to fully explore the effects of increasing or decreasing your prices. You will need to ensure that your model is sophisticated enough to accommodate the effects of winning or losing sales to your competitors based on pricing alone.

Are we selling benefits or products?

Benefits every time! Take a look at your sales literature or your existing website. Be honest, what do you see first – benefits or product names? In the first paragraph of every product description, is there more about the product or about the benefits? Have you kept the benefits simple?

Customers invariably want more. They want to do more, own more, achieve more. But they don't want to do it themselves. They want you to do it. They believe that, if they buy something from you, it will help them in their quest for more. No matter whether they are a business or consumer, they have an expectation – they expect something from you.

In return, you make a promise. You promise to supply them not with the product that they want but with the satisfaction that they expect. The product or service is merely a vehicle for that satisfaction. In other words, customers buy benefits.

It's impossible to separate the benefits from the product or service when we consider the usefulness – or value – of a purchase. That's why, when we measure value, we take account of both:

Value = functional benefits (what the product does) × perceived benefits (the satisfaction of your promise) × relative price

So how do we focus on benefits? Well, if you sell shelves, you're selling tidiness. If you sell haircuts, you're selling hope. If you sell accountancy, you're selling peace of mind. If you sell human-resources consultancy, you're selling productivity. There's always a benefit to every product. The trick is to sell the benefit, then the product.

Before you start thinking about your website, you might like to revisit your sales-and-marketing messages. You might like to consider emphasising the benefits. In fact, you might like to revisit the benefits themselves. Here's a useful five-step guide:

1 What benefits do we currently offer, for each product or service? Try to use single words such as 'profit', 'power' or 'growth' for businesses and 'health', 'prestige' or 'excitement' for consumers.
2 What benefits should we be offering? Do we currently offer enough? Do our competitors' products offer more benefits? Do our competitors' reputations imply more benefit?
3 What headline messages explain each benefit in fewer than ten

words? Apply this to every benefit and every product or service you offer.

4   What changes should we make to existing products or services to genuinely offer these benefits? What kind of new products will deliver the new benefits? How quickly can we launch them?

5   Where are the best places to sell these benefits on a website, without overdoing it? (You might consider the homepage, the product or service pages and the catalogue or order pages.)

How far ahead should we be?

Try to imagine a perfect company – a perfect version of your own business. You have permanently delighted and 100 per cent loyal customers. No one ever defects to the competition, who have become a major source of business for you. Every month, you turn your 100 per cent strike-rate marketing programme on a new competitor. You just pick off the biggest and best customers. No one ever leaves the staff – they just self-learn, self-train and self-improve. Your suppliers constantly work at actively improving the value they offer you, without your lifting a finger or raising your voice. Productivity constantly creeps up every month, as management devises ever more efficient ways of doing things. And at the centre of it all is your world-beating e-Commerce site, feeding your customers with spiralling value, your production team with very precise orders and your management with crystal-clear analysis.

Now work back through that list. What effort and cost will it take to achieve each of these? What's the gap between reality now and a perfect future? Here's a little help:

Outcome	Action Required
delighted customers	great product
low customer defection	great customer service
competitor feed you	superb sales, superb product
100 per cent sales-strike rate	competitive attitude, superb value
self-improving staff	learning environment
suppliers increasing value	collaborative supplier relations
productivity gradient	good internal communication and managers
world-beating website	proactive web team
spiralling value	innovation programme
very precise orders	good teamwork on web design
crystal-clear analysis	marketing, not technology, thinking

And I'm sure you could go on adding to the list. Of course, every company is different. And for every company the cost of the action is different. But you can easily work through a rough guide, such as the table above, to calculate the approximate cost or effort of improvement and compare it with the value of their results. From there, it's easy to prioritise, and work out how far ahead you should be.

In preparing your thoughts and resources for an e-Commerce project, you should address these issues – even if lightly – at the outset. Because, if you don't, you'll be redesigning your site after you have addressed them. New sales processes, new customer-service processes and new innovation processes will all result in redesigning the site.

Digitising conventional products and services

Every product or service you intend for e-Commerce should have an online version of itself. Even a haircut can be lovingly described, illustrated and individually priced on the net! The trick is approaching your real-world product with a view to making an online version of it. And that usually involves 'digital wrappers'.

What is a digital wrapper?

It's a combination of copy, images, functionality, promotions and processes that are attached to a real product or service, in order to help you sell it online. Often, it helps if you can bundle related products or services to increase value as well.

At first glance this looks like nothing more than a description of the product. But in fact it's much more. It's the task of carefully making your product or service seem at home on the Internet. Take a look at these illustrations.

Digital wrapper for jewellery

Greg is launching a new online shop for his wife's silversmith work. She's a budding artist and is growing her reputation for unusual and romantic bracelets. She works in silver, and they want to reach an international audience. Greg's digital wrappers are:

- Superb three-zoom options on the photos of the jewellery he has taken with his digital camera (normal, close and superclose detail)
- The ability to see the same bracelet against different-colour shirtsleeves so customers can be more certain of their choice
- Poetic descriptions of the bracelets, with drill-down links to very detailed descriptions of the design and fabrication process (for those who want detail)

- Removal of the shopping-basket interface to emphasise the one-off, bespoke nature of the product
- Bundled free good-luck, insignia or alphabet charm (cleverly worked into the price)
- Free membership of the romantic-prose group, which publishes online once a month
- 10 per cent discount for those who submit to the discussion group a creative description of the romantic effect of the bracelet
- 24-hour dispatch
- An online competition for the best romantic-prose story, submitted to the discussion group

Digital wrapper for management consultancy

Fiona is preparing her company's new website for their environmental consultancy services. She wants to reach large companies in five key UK industries and public-sector organisations. Her digital wrappers are:

- Drill-down descriptions of the benefits of environmental compliance, starting with a single word (e.g. 'savings'), then a single paragraph, then a page of detail (again, those who seek detail can get it, while it is not forced on those who don't)
- An online two-minute environmental audit, with follow-through sales promotion
- A target measure of energy efficiency for the five target industries measured in cost per employee
- A high-security extranet for clients so they can manage their account, order top-up services, review the consultancy reports and analysis online and compare themselves against benchmarks
- A free membership service that publishes an online monthly guide to regulation and savings (but requires research information to be submitted)
- A checklist of the top ten most common inefficiencies in the UK (based on the membership research above) and a simple 'how-to' button-based quiz that solves them online
- Photographs of the consultants, with CV summaries and downloadable longer CVs
- A light-hearted 'green-gain' page where previous clients describe their green work and its superb results
- A serious discussion group that allows corporates to discuss waste, pollution, energy and environmental issues anonymously

Digital wrapper for office-cleaning company

Hamish runs a small office-cleaning business, and wants to win extra sales in the Glasgow area. His company specialises in tower-block window cleaning, and he wants to secure thirty new contracts with landlords within six months. His digital wrappers are:

- Quick-cost calculator based on number of floors and floorspace to help customers estimate their window-cleaning and office-cleaning costs
- Light-hearted 'clean this window' visual game, where visitors have to control a basket of window cleaners to just the right height to be able to see through the window at a Glasgow skyline
- Simple enquiry form for potential clients to order a three-month trial
- 10 per cent discount for all customers who order and maintain their account online
- A simple cross-selling device that suggests office cleaning services when customers enquire about a trial three-month window-cleaning account
- An email-based report issued after every job, describing and showing digital photos of the repair of the outside of the building to its landlord
- Website artwork to include office-block photos with shiny clean windows
- Simple descriptions of the service, with drill-down links to photos of the cleaning team and details of the environmental benefits of the cleaning products (again these are not forced: they are for customers who want to dig deeper)

The pitfalls of going online

If you're tackling e-Commerce for the first time, it's likely that you're being driven by a rush of enthusiasm and a passion for the new. Beware! Plenty of entrepreneurial projects wind up on the scrap heap because caution wasn't exercised. Before you implement your big idea, run through a reality check.

Thinking too big

- You can triple your market share within twelve months. Very ambitious.
- You can change the industry within three years. Very unlikely.
- You can swallow your suppliers or competitors. Rarely.
- You can create a new kind of customer. Almost never.

Try to reduce your grand plan to more achievable goals, and keep a close watch on profit and productivity.

Thinking too small

You may counter the last pitfall with overly modest goals. There are still plenty of unclaimed stakes out there in the e-Commerce landscape. Every month, in my office, we meet at least two clients who have found a niche in which there is simply zero competition. So take a good look at the competition and, if it's poor, consider raising your game and gunning for market leadership within three years.

Thinking too tech

- You need to understand technology. Not so.
- You need to have an IT department. You don't.
- You need whizzy hi-tech features on your site. Not if your customers don't like it.
- You need big back-office systems or an intranet. Not if you're working on a tight budget.

Try to keep the technology out of your thinking and planning, especially in the early stages of the project. Focus on activities, value, processes and benefits instead.

Thinking too conventional

You may have fallen in love with a competitor site. You may have found the perfect interface, the perfect design, the perfect business model. And the temptation is to copy. Don't! Adapt the idea and make it better.

Break a few rules at least. Forge your online business in your own mould, use your own approach. Why? Because it's more likely you'll have strong convictions about the site. And it's more likely to be unique or noticeably different.

Going too slowly

Don't approach e-Commerce as you would any other project. It's not another project. It's more like a new way of trading. Maybe you're pretty quick at getting new things up and running. But the game here is rushing safely. There's more on this in Chapter 10.

The better your business idea, the more reason to do it quickly, to be the first. The key time here is after the research is complete. As soon as your analysis is in, that's when the clock starts ticking, and you really don't want much more than three months between analysis and launch. Otherwise, your site is out of date before it's live!

No pain no gain

Now that we've explored fully how e-Commerce applies to your business, where the pitfalls lie, and many of the acid tests, let's look forward a little: what lies ahead for you as you take the plunge?

Certainly your management will lose a significant chunk of their diary in the early stages of the project. That will probably mean working longer hours or deferring some day-to-day or week-to-week decision making. If you're leading this project, try making it your responsibility to keep motivation high and disruption to a minimum.

After the initial flurry is over, there will be a lull, while the site is under construction, when nothing seems to happen. This is the best time for management to catch up with other projects that were deferred while the web project kicked off.

After the site launches, you may experience low initial sales returns. Indeed, after the site has been running for a while – maybe six months – you may still be experiencing lower sales returns. Be prepared for this. Hopefully, your revenue model was not overambitious and your expectations not too high. You should prepare contingency sales plans, which you should be comfortable with implementing almost at the drop of hat. One of the best sales strategies on the Internet is 'fire, aim, fire, aim'.

You may also experience low staff enthusiasm for the site, even if you have pushed out a vigorous campaign to involve all staff with its launch. Dissent may surface from some of the most unusual quarters: the technology team, the operations team – even sales! Maybe you raised their hopes too high. Maybe they wanted pictures on the site. Maybe they're scared that their jobs will change. Anticipate these reactions. Prepare to spend time – more time than you think is necessary – winning over the hearts and minds of your staff. After all, once the site is live you will depend on their enthusiasm and their knowledge of the site in selling it to existing customers.

Are you ready for all that pain? You're still up for it? Chapter 3 explains the prevailing rules of Internet Marketing.

CHAPTER THREE

Learn the rules of marketing in e-Commerce

1 Internet marketing is 90 per cent product, 10 per cent perception

In the late nineties, websites were about image. Now, most seasoned web users *expect* image. What differentiates at the present (at least for the next twelve months, as far as we can predict!) is the quality and depth of the site and its products. That means choice, functionality and quality of the products and information on your site. This includes the catalogue, how-to guides, demos, interactivity and humour. So the key differentiator is online product – making sure that what customers can do is different.

This has little to do with design or presentation – and everything to do with content. So your first port of call in applying this rule is to the operational team, not the marketing or sales people. Then work backwards to the marketing team, focusing on pricing, distribution and delivery, and finally presentation.

2 Your e-customers are your sales team

E-customers have the upper hand. They can shop around much more easily than in the real world. And, with shopping e-malls and price-comparing shop-bots proliferating, they can compare more easily, too.

But, when they're delighted, they can tell a thousand other like-minded customers in discussion forums. Word of mouth (or word of web) is very powerful in Internet sales. So accept the power that customers have, and work with it. You can't *push* your messages at e-customers: you have to let them *pull* info from your site. Consider creating an easy-to-use area for their views on your site, evolving your sales materials so they have a stronger bias towards customer referrals and success stories.

The successful e-business is likely to have a broad and enthusiastic community of satisfied customers, which has been harnessed for commercial advantage.

3 Customers buy benefits and proofs

See things the way your customer sees them – try to re-create their experience. As the saying goes, if you want to understand a red Indian spend a day walking in his moccasins.

Customers have low attention spans – just as you do when you visit a supplier's site. Customers are impatient. They may be uneducated in the use of your site. But above all they'll have a little 'benefit alarm', a little device that triggers when they've spotted 'something in it for me'.

So think 'what's in it for me?' (WIIFM?) when you prepare your marketing. As producers we get preoccupied with what we put into the product (in other words, the features rather than the benefits).

Customers are much more interested in what is in it for them (they focus on benefits) and how the site can demonstrate these benefits (the proofs). Every page on your website should paraphrase the words 'Which means that . . .' to ensure that you are explaining how your product will solve your customer's problem.

4 Prepare to compete and be more aggressive

The effect of competition tends to be more marked on the Internet, especially for smaller businesses. If you work in one, you may be familiar with a competitive but not aggressive market – perhaps competing on service or product features. With e-Commerce, you may need to compete on a more vigorous basis: '10 per cent cheaper than www.competitor.com' or 'over 300 products more to choose from than any other UK website'.

When you put your business online, even if the competition seems benign, have a set of rock-solid competitive strategies up your sleeve, ready to attack when provoked.

5 Internet business returns are long-term

e-Commerce is a long-term game. Don't dabble. Do it properly, invest wisely and don't expect payback for around 12 months.

It's wise to think big before starting up an e-Commerce programme – take a broad view and work out what you're prepared to give up now in the way of cash, your time and your staff energies in order to get a good long-term success.

Also, there's no getting away from it – rushing in quickly for short-term gains may spoil your opportunities (not to mention damage your investment budget) in the longer-term game. If you rush out a cheap and nasty site, with poor delivery and poor customer service, you may make a quick buck from novelty interest. And you may have spent 60 per cent of your entire year's web budget in doing so.

It's much better to work in smaller, well-planned phases, so you can inch up customer service and delivery in parallel with the site's development.

6 Your affiliates are also your sales team

Affiliates are powerful allies. If you choose your affiliate wisely, you can double or treble the success of your site. This can be in terms of traffic, new customers, new sales enquiries or new purchases.

Identifying appropriate affiliates is relatively easy. The hard work comes in negotiating and drafting contracts with them. Usually, an affiliate will be looking to you for high-quality content which they could not easily generate themselves. And usually you will be able to secure a discreet branding deal, whereby the affiliate will not only carry your content on their site but will also mention or endorse your brand.

Of course, there's no such thing as a free lunch. You may have to pay royalties or share revenue with your affiliate, but it's a sure-fire way of piggybacking on the success of others in order to grow your business quickly.

7 Internet marketing comes from the whole company, not just sales

If the sales people are the only ones carrying the web marketing flag, you're in trouble! If the sales people are the only ones with email or Internet access, or if they're busy dealing with the boom caused by your new site, how will customers get service? Customers will place orders, only to find that delivery dates, customer service or just simple confirmation and thank-you notes are disappointingly late. And what if there's a query on a purchase, a complaint, a change of order? Are you going to push all that through to sales, who probably won't be in any position to act, other than as an intermediary?

Plan and relate the key business activities for the whole company around the customer and their approach to buying from you. Educate your production or operations people, your office manager and your receptionist so that they understand their role in putting the customer first. At the very least, that means convenience, speed, hospitality, choice, proactivity, manners and honesty.

8 Be different – be your own Number One

Being different is what a large part of marketing communications is all about. Of course, when we say 'different', we often mean 'better'. And how can you be better if the market leader is lower in price, stronger on service and richer in advanced product features?

Be Number One in your own, self-defined category. In a field of one, you're the top player! If the market leader is known for price, service and choice, don't compete on those grounds. Pick your own terrain – innovation, style or location, for example. 'We're Number One for modern, stylish work in city X' would be a good start. This is called positioning.

Often, your competitors' positioning will be unclear. Good! This gives you more choice when you pick a territory. Monitor your competitors' sites. Work out their implied market positions. Then map out a differentiated position. Change your colours, your language tone, your offers, your products – everything – to match your chosen positioning, to show how much better and different you are.

9 The management team drives e-Commerce

You won't pull off miraculous improvements from anywhere else! Drive all your Internet business programmes from the management team. Sure, get everybody involved – but make it your priority to drive the programme from the top. Otherwise other priorities will take over, practical hurdles will get in the way and your marketing and web development will sink in a swamp of mediocrity.

You'll need good advisers if you're not web-savvy yourself. You'll need good leadership skills, listening skills and Herculean patience. You're about to do some pretty upside-down things – things that the existing company was never designed for – so expect resistance from people, systems and culture.

10 Success and failure are both necessary

Failure is definitely a part of learning. It's estimated that between 70 and 80 per cent of all Internet start-ups will fail within their first two years of trading in the UK, depending on which pundit you talk to. In the USA in 1999, the receivership industry established itself firmly in Silicon Valley, and has ever since been buying up distressed enterprises and asset-stripping them. The industry is headed towards Europe next.

But, on the other hand, if you don't fail occasionally then you're not taking enough risks. Especially on the Internet!

First, try to minimise the opportunity for failure by researching, testing and planning your site before you launch it. Control your budget, and put aside a limited contingency budget to tackle problems before the whole project collapses in failure.

Second, when you do encounter failure, recognise it early and cut your losses before disaster ensues. Modify immediately your failed campaigns, your unpopular website, your overeager emails.

Finally, don't get depressed! Pick yourself up off the ground, get straight back on the horse and ride!

11 Flexible teams, not departments

Try to break down the walls between departments. This is one of the biggest and most common barriers to good service and swift delivery in e-Commerce. Right now, you may have clear-cut and quite effective paperwork systems. They may define nicely the responsibilities and time scales for different departments in the processing of a customer order. But they probably also divide rather than unite your staff in handling the task. They may involve departments or fixed teams, where only one individual may need to be involved. Quite possibly, this will need to change.

You don't need staff working to departmental priorities or waiting for the paperwork to arrive before serving the customer. If you're going to increase your speed, you're going to need members of staff from all over the company to work in small, temporary and flexible teams – and quickly – on key tasks, such as order processing, handling complaints, winning new customers and developing new products.

12 Product life is shorter than you think

Just about every product will eventually go through a life cycle – a sequence of stages including idea, creation, launch, growth, revision, further growth, maturity and decline. This is especially true with information products, but also applies to physical and service products. You can try to extend or reinvigorate any particular phase, but the life cycle will eventually prevail.

Understanding the life cycle allows you to manage your product or service, to know when to be thinking about phasing out old products and when to phase in new ones without cannibalising existing sales.

13 Speed doesn't kill

Internet marketing is like conventional marketing speeded up. Customers expect replies more quickly, delivery more quickly. 'Instant' is the byword. So how quick is your business now? Can you drive up your operating speeds? Where are your bottlenecks? Where can you improve speed most easily?

Making changes to speed means making changes to working practices and ultimately to workplace culture (see the next few rules). So tread carefully – you don't want a revolt on your hands. You can phase in speed changes, so the effect is gradual on staff, but sufficiently improved to meet customer expectations by the time the new site goes live.

The goal here for most businesses delivering from orders taken via the Internet is to cut dispatch from 28 days to 2–3 days at the maximum, unless you've got a very tolerant customer community.

14 Feedback means knowledge – feed-forward means profit

One of the easiest ways to put the customer first is to ask questions continually (and to respect the customer's answers!). Online, you offer them clusters of choices, not lengthy questionnaires. Back it up with conventional phone calls and meetings. The more you ask, the more competitive advantage you can create, and the stronger your customer relationships become.

But knowledge is no use on its own. Feedback is simply a feed of views back to you. Value, differentiation and competitive advantage count only when they're at your customer's door – when you've fed them forward. So be sure to have formal mechanisms or systems in place to feed forward. These may include a twelve-week innovation cycle, a monthly product revision meeting, or the management team increasing the target for sales from new products to 25 per cent.

And nothing succeeds in cementing customer relations like advice heeded – just watch your customers' reactions to a new product or feature that they suggested!

15 Don't just measure stats – interpret them

Sure, measure all you can – an objective isn't worth the paper it's written on if you can't track your progress towards it. But don't be a hit counter. Analyse the results – then interpret them for meaningful trends or comparisons. For instance, '48 per cent increase in traffic to the after-sales care area' may be interpreted as 'the product needs tweaking, and customers want stronger relationships'.

Also, measure the right things. It's amazing how many companies don't. If your business depends on advertising revenues from high volumes of traffic, then obviously it makes sense to measure traffic. However, if your business depends on winning new customers, then you should be measuring new customer registrations, first-time visitors or first-time purchases.

16 The 80/20 rule – cut back on rubbish, focus on the juicy bits

Pareto's 80/20 Principle is everywhere we look: 80 per cent of profits come from 20 per cent of customers; 80 per cent of the website gets 20 per cent of the visits, and, conversely 20 per cent of profits would come from 80 per cent of customers. If you want to work more smartly, focus on the highly effective and ignore the rest!

Draw a line below your top 20 per cent profit-producing customers and review the rest for their profit level. Consider introducing new prices to raise margins with these customers. Some will 'play the game', which is great for profit, and maybe a little tricky for a while for customer relations. But the others may be reluctant to pay you enough for profit. So now you can ask yourself a question: Why are we keeping these customers at all?

You may also like to analyse the characteristics of your top 20 per cent customers – perhaps they're in markets, channels or locations that have something in common. If you can establish a pattern, tap the seam and go after more, similarly profitable customers.

17 Attach the right people to Internet marketing

You wouldn't ask an electrician to design your shop window, would you? So don't ask just *any* IT people to design your website! Make sure the message makers and the product/service-delivery people are engaged fully in the site.

Assemble a well-balanced team to get the site live, and expect to make changes to the team once it starts to operate. Qualifications for team membership are web-savviness, enthusiasm, customer focus and a desire to change the world.

Don't make do with senior people who don't fit the bill. And don't give too much influence to technologists.

18 Look again at the 4 Ps of marketing

Conventional marketing is based on the four Ps of products, price, promotion and place (or distribution and access). There are a few key issues that belong to each of these Ps:

- **Product:** should be dripping with information – pictures, text or stats
- **Promotion:** best when offline and online efforts are integrated and stronger if underpinned by word of mouth
- **Price:** should be more dynamic and opportunistic than in the offline-only world
- **Place:** distribution of product should be 2–3 days max, and access to staff or help desk should be 12 hours min, 24 hours ideally

You should also consider three extra special Ps just for luck:

- **People:** just as online as your customers
- **Processes:** more important and better defined than your departments – and based around key tasks that your customers experience, such as ordering, choosing, receiving
- **Privacy:** respect customer privacy and your customer will respect your commerce

HOW TO DO e-COMMERCE

The virtuous spiral

To do e-Commerce, your business should follow a virtuous spiral. When the preparations finish, and the site is properly launched, you should commit to a continuous programme of review and innovation. When you become proficient at e-Commerce, you'll be pushing out the spiral ever further, creating more growth and more profit.

Assuming that you're starting from nothing, you'll need to follow a set of self-dependent activities. The sequence may appear to be obvious – indeed it is – but if you stick to it, you will reap the rewards of good preparation.

In this section of the book, we explain how to tackle each of these phases in simple practical steps.

CHAPTER FOUR

Assemble your best, best team

Everything in business starts with people. e-Commerce is no different. You need to assemble three kinds of team members – staff, advisers and partners.

Involve the best senior staff

Bring together your best people and, right from the start, accept that this project will demand their time and will reduce their capacity to fulfil their normal roles.

When you assemble this team, do it once and once only. You don't need failed starts in a project like this. Choose senior people – movers and shakers, not juniors or greenhorns. You wouldn't invite low-calibre staff to join the board, would you? This project is as important. This is the project start-up team that will take you from nowhere to your first serious trading site. And they'll need a holiday when their job is done!

After the site is live, you'll probably need a different team to run it – people with strong customer and innovation skills. But, to get this important project off the ground, you should make an effort to recruit a good balanced team. You should consider the following types of individual:

Team member	Role	Other role
Chair: Open-minded, fair, neutral, motivator, not dazed by technology	Getting the best out of every member of the team, supporting a balance of creativity and pragmatism	Generating enthusiasm and anticipation in the company
Customer: Yes, the customer! Put your closest customer on the team, or at least represent her, by using a sales person	To explain what she wants, in her own words	None
Maverick: Sparky, irrepressible rebel who wants to break the mould	Creating new ideas for competitive advantage, web presentation, customer feedback, production processes, distribution and any other area that's important to your business	Drawing inspiration from industry sites, award-winning sites, competitor sites and supplier sites
Floor manager: Solid, intelligent developer of other people's ideas with good understanding of production & operations	Developing the creative's ideas into workable solutions. Drawing up simple change plans to the production or operations part of the business	Consulting with production or operations people so they feel involved in the preparations for e-Commerce
Detective: Well-connected, encyclopaedic detective who knows where to look for people, suppliers, and partners	Preparing outline budgets and work schedules. Briefing and inviting partner organisations and specialists to join the team for guest slots	Identifying and recruiting the right partner organisations for web construction, distribution, affiliate promotions, e-Commerce advisers, design and, where appropriate, government funding

Team member	Role	Other role
Cash police: Rational, probably financial expert	Ensuring value for money is the goal from Day 1	Asking hard questions. Seeing that both short- and long-term returns are optimised. Consulting with senior staff not on the team on budget and revenue matters

Note that there is no technology person on this team. Why? Is it because we want our aspirations to drive this site, not technology? Yes, but that's not the real reason. Is it because technical people tend to dominate? Actually it's almost the opposite. Most of us are nontechnical people. We have a tendency to become weak in the presence of software engineers (or confused!). And some of us regard e-Commerce as only a technology issue, not a commercial one (give them a copy of this book for a quick remedy!). Consequently, we tend to flatten our aspirations and defer to technical thinking. This is the worst possible starting point for an e-Commerce project.

Incidentally, this is no slight on the technologist, many of whom now have excellent business skills: they have a crucial role to play during the planning and building stages of the project. But, unless you have every confidence in your team's ability to stay focused on commerce in the presence of software engineers, it's best to pull techies in on an as-needs basis.

Don't be scared to put someone else in the chair position if you're a creative or an innovator yourself. The team will work best with the right balance, which may not necessarily reflect your current job functions.

Get good e-Commerce advisers

Don't try e-Commerce for the first time without an 'e-adult' present, unless you're supremely confident! Even if you're paying only for a sounding-board service rather than full-on consultancy, it's always good to build experience into the team. Most e-Commerce consultants work for web-design agencies and will be gunning for a 'design-and-build' contract, off the back of their consultancy. This is no bad thing, since they'll steer towards what they know can be built, and hence you'll get real-world, pragmatic advice from the outset. However, it may be sensible to separate the advice contract from the design-and-build contract. You may find that, after your strategy and planning work, you require specialised services that your adviser's company cannot supply, such as multilingual text, database engines or third-party data feeds.

So how do you recruit a good e-Commerce adviser? In no particular order, here are the options:

- [ ] Use the adviser that another business recommends.
- [ ] Contact your local Small Business Service or Business Link office and ask for a list of approved e-consultants.
- [ ] Get in touch with your trade organisation or other business organisation such as the Department of Trade and Industry, your local chamber of commerce, the Chartered Institute of Marketing or your local enterprise agency. They will be likely to supply you with a list of recognised or familiar e-consultants.
- [ ] Call your own web host or any major business host such as www.netlink.co.uk, or www.magic-moments.com.
- [ ] Look in Internet magazines (*Internet Works*, for example) at the listings, usually in the rear of the magazine. You can also search online (try www.iwks.com).
- [ ] Contact the Institute of Directors, Institute of Management Consultants or the British Accreditation Bureau and ask for a list of approved e-consultants.

What telltale signs indicate quality in an e-consultant?

- [ ] Listening more than talking
- [ ] Awareness of return on investment
- [ ] Lots of questions about how you currently do business
- [ ] Experience and good client referrals
- [ ] Marketing or commercial (not technical) background
- [ ] Good communicator

Recruit reliable partners

Now you've decided on your staff team and possibly an e-consultant, you should consider at least one of several kinds of partners – visual (web) designers, web constructors, distribution companies and marketing affiliates. Each plays its part in delivering success to your door.

Visual web designers

Design is subjective. By its very nature everyone will have a different opinion on good design and bad design. However, there is such a thing as *appropriate* design. And 'appropriate' is usually more objective than subjective. But just what is appropriate?

Appropriate design takes into account four key factors:

- The audience – their visual literacy
- Your business – its image and reputation
- Your product or service – its complexity or simplicity
- Your competitors – their design standards

When you set about designing a site, or commissioning a designer, the audience really must come first. If they're elderly or very young, simple images may be more appropriate. If they are aged 15–25, they are more likely to identify with complex and more modern imagery. If the target audience is well educated, then perhaps classical or historical imagery might be better received than, say, pop or TV culture imagery.

After the audience has been thought about, it's a good idea to consider your company's reputation and its current image. Clearly, if you're already known as an aggressive kind of business, passive, calm, soothing images will be inappropriate. If you already have a reputation for, say, innovation, then traditional images, such as portraits of the chairman, will convey a conflicting message.

Next, consider your product or service. If you make clocks, clearly imagery that conveys a sense of time, precision or engineering will be appropriate, whereas images that imply randomness or vagueness may very well be inappropriate.

Finally, do look at your competitors' sites. You'll probably find that many of them are inappropriate (to your great joy!). But it's worth trying to work out which ones are appropriate and deciding which parts of them are a useful model for your own site and which parts of them must be clearly differentiated against.

Here's a list of visual design considerations before you embark on commissioning a visual designer:

- [ ] Planning – is there evidence of good planning work? In particular, check that they ask questions on audience, reputation, time frame, and ask to see their normal planning documents.
- [ ] Simplicity – in their previous work, how have they used spaciousness, especially in large complex sites. Sites that are jam-packed with links, flashing images and scrolling messages are generally very hard to absorb and don't usually go down well with regular visitors.
- [ ] Navigation – is there evidence of consistency and intuitive location of regularly used features in the navigation system? The hardest-to-use system is the one that changes on every page.

☐ Interaction – is there evidence of imaginative use of interactive features in their previous work? In particular, look for buttons, images and animation that react to user input.

☐ Creativity and originality – is there evidence of striking, genuinely original artwork in their previous efforts? Try to get a consensus of use among your own staff before deciding on this.

☐ Compatibility – is there evidence that their previous work is compatible with all browsers? This may seem like a trivial question, but it's a dead giveaway on their technical competence.

Web constructors

Here you face a big question. Build the site in-house or use web specialists? This largely depends on whether or not you wish to control your own destiny by relying on partner companies. Some entrepreneurs feel the need to own every part of the business process, while others are comfortable subcontracting parts such as delivery, packaging or even core parts of the product or service. You're the best judge of this, but here's a little tool to help you decide.

Web constructor	Pros	Cons
Web agency	• Experience • Objective • Broad range of skills • Production speed • Libraries of prewritten features • Up-to-date on technology	• Reliance on third party • Not always the best e-consultants • Sometimes sausage-machine approach
Create team in-house	• Increases capabilities and skills in-house • Increases company and management awareness of e-Commerce • Dedicated team • Flexibility without extra costs	• Can be costly • Hard to recruit or retain good people (high mobility in labour market) • Low speed of production

A third option

There another option to web construction – DIY. Now this one is risky. Without the back-up of experienced staff or a web agency, you may make costly mistakes. However, it can be done. It involves using tools you're possibly unfamiliar with, and learning 'on the job'. Here are a few software options:

Web authoring software

This is the software that you use to build and lay out the site. You can combine text, pictures, navigation, tables, forms, basic interactivity and links with these kinds of packages. Among the best are Dreamweaver (www.macromedia.com) and GoLive (www.adobe.com), with FrontPage 2000 (www.Microsoft.com) a reasonable contender.

Catalogue software

You'll need a secure catalogue to load your products or services into. This is the master copy of everything that's for sale on your site. At the low end of the scale, Shopcreator Stall (www. shopcreator.com) is cheap and simple. In the middle, Actinic Catalogue (www.actinic.com) is a good, flexible package which requires reasonable technical skills. And at the top of the range, Enfinity (www.intershop.com) and iShop (www.oracle.com) provide heavy-weight catalogue functionality.

Artwork software

You'll need to create images of your products and probably some corporate artwork too (such as decorative, navigation and background images). These packages allow you to tint, stretch, crop, blow up and manipulate your pictures in almost any way imaginable. Fireworks (www.macromedia.com), Photoshop (www.adobe.com) and PhotoPaint (www.corel.com) are among the best, but Paintshop Pro (www.jasc.com) comes pretty close.

Animation software

Animation tends to generate huge files, which require long download times. Until we all have cheap, fast, broadband connections to the Internet, the main options for animation are Flash (www.macromedia.com) and animated gifs, produced by packages such as CorelPaint (www.corel.com). There's always streaming video, but now we're getting a little overambitious for DIY.

File Transfer Protocol (uploading) software

Once you've built your site on your local PC or Mac, you need to upload it to your web host. FTP is the way we do this. Dreamweaver already has this built in, but, if you need separate FTP, you can hardly go wrong with the shareware package Cute FTP (www.download.com).

Choose appropriate distribution companies

When the customer finally gets the goods she has ordered, three major components of marketing reach closure:

> ☐ Exchange – money and goods are swapped.
> ☐ Satisfaction – only now does the customer fully believe your promise.
> ☐ Loyalty – only now is the customer willing to make a repeat purchase or recommend you by word of mouth or web.

All this depends on delivery. Not on sales or image, not on website or production. Delivery. That's a big burden for a seemingly minor activity. So ask yourself two big questions:

> ☐ Is this a burden we want?
> ☐ Can we do better than say DHL or UPS?

If you can answer 'yes' to both, then you should keep distribution in-house. If not, as is the case with most companies, then seriously consider outsourcing.

So how should you choose a distribution partner? Here's a checklist for any potential partner:

Delivery service feature	DHL	Parcel Force	Now Now Now	Omega Express	Your Partner
Deliver to businesses	Y	Y	Y	Y	?
Deliver to Consumers	Y	Y	Y	Y	?
Global	Y				?
National	Y	Y		Y	?
Go to inner city areas	Y		Y	Y	?
Same day	Y		Y	Y	?
Next day	Y	Y	Y	Y	?
Early or late deliveries			Y	Y	?
Integrate with your e-Commerce system	Y				?
Flexible on price (up to 25% discount)	Y		Y	Y	?
Low-cost insurance available	Y	Y	Y	Y	?
Accepts your fragile goods as packed OK	Y		Y	Y	?

The web addresses for these businesses are as follows:

- www.dhl.co.uk
- www.parcelforce.co.uk
- www.nownownow.co.uk
- www.securicor.co.uk/omegaexpress

Now you've identified a good partner, what sort of contract do you want? Here are five useful clauses to insist on:

- three-month trial period
- 25 per cent discount for sole-supplier status
- Delivery times to suit your customers
- Returned goods at a lower rate
- Partner approves your packing methods and accepts that they render your goods fit for dispatch (so you can't be blamed for damage in transit)

Government funding

If you're a small to medium-sized enterprise, you've got a good chance of winning subsidy from the government to part-pay for the costs of these third parties.

The government's Small Business Service (SBS) will, under certain conditions, provide funding for up to half of your project costs. You'll probably have to work with a government-recognised partner who has been pre-qualified. Check out the DTI website for details of funding.

What to tell non-team members

The first thing you should do when you embark on a major web project is to communicate clearly a positive message about the website to all staff. Most staff are suspicious of change – they fear it might replace their jobs, or in some way negatively impact on their working lives. Staff who work in the production or operational side of the business will probably need a little more reassurance. After all, it's they who will be hit the hardest. Almost certainly they will need to change their working practices – probably by working a faster system, or by creating new products or services.

You also need to keep the IT department feeling involved. This may sound strange, but if you are approaching a project correctly you'll probably have very few technical staff on the project team. While this may help you to keep focused on commerce, you've got to keep the IT department feeling special – feeling specialist. This means being patient with some of the propeller heads who work in the IT department – listening to them, bothering to understand them and being sensitive to their strange requirements. These are usually working very antisocial hours and drinking cups of real coffee! Cut them some slack – you need them on your site.

It's usually a good idea to set up secondary teams to focus on specific major tasks within the main project. These may include a production/operations team, which would focus on changes to working practices in the core part of the business, a marketing team to focus on promoting the site and setting up affiliate partners, and a finance team to control costs and funding.

What goes wrong when the team is wrong

When you embark on e-Commerce, your company is making history. Not only is it sailing into uncharted territory, it's also laying down the foundations for what may be major change. It's a good idea to appreciate this fact when recruiting your web team (it's also a good idea to keep returning to the fact that you're making history during the web project itself!) Why? Because it's very easy to see the web project as a small IT programme rather than as a major overhaul of the entire business. Two companies I worked with recently underestimated the importance of e-Commerce to their short- and medium-term future. As a consequence, they underinvested their time and their resources. Their web teams became ineffective and consequently their websites did too.

So what can go wrong? The pitfalls usually occur in a number of areas:

- Inadequate skills – the management team is simply not web-savvy enough to manage the project, resulting in poor decisions and usually inappropriate designs and content for the intended audiences
- Inadequate budget – the management team approaches budgeting cautiously, resulting in a dated-looking, uncompetitive site to which customers react badly
- Offline thinking – the management team approaches the project as if it were putting up a new building, resulting in lengthy research, lengthy decision making and a site that is six months behind everyone else
- One-off thinking – the management team regards the web project as having a beginning, middle and end, resulting in a website that never varies, and from which regular visitors eventually turn away
- Technology approach – the management team delegates the web project to the IT department, which promptly creates a site that delivers no commercial benefits whatsoever

- Navel-gazing – the management team listens very closely to the web team, but fails to monitor competitor sites, resulting in a website that cannot defend against competitor action
- No offline programme – the management team forgets to integrate changes to sales, marketing communications, order handling, production and customer service during the project, resulting in a bodged, bolt-on approach which no employee or department is happy with

So what?

You've made a good start. You've pulled together a team, on which you will depend in the coming months, and on which your business will depend in the coming years! You've identified partners and advisers and you've explained the project and involved everyone in the company.

Chapter checklist

Do I have the following?

- [ ] A well-balanced web project team
- [ ] Good e-Commerce advisers
- [ ] Reliable partners for design, construction, distribution
- [ ] A promising list of affiliates for channel marketing
- [ ] Staff who are informed and comfortable with this web project

CHAPTER FIVE

Classify your e-customers, and spy on competitors

To open the research phase, we need an e-customer survey, rigorous segmentation, a detailed review of at least ten other sites that you like, and a competitor analysis.

Let's start with the marketplace. We can kick off with the needs and behaviour of customers and competitors. This is less daunting than it may appear.

How do you understand what customers want when you don't even know who they are? And how do you assess what competitors are up to when you have the names of only a few of them? You may be feeling particularly anxious about answering these questions if you have no website at present.

Not every e-customer is unique

Not a popular view among e-gurus, but it's true. People like to belong – to groups of other like-minded people. And, if people like to belong to groups, then you should try to make the most of this, by recognising their differences and customising your products or services, your pricing and your communications to suit them. The starting point here is segmentation.

Segmentation is the business of dividing your market into smaller segments. Each segment has similar characteristics and can therefore be treated as a separate market in its own right. Why bother? Why not just treat everyone the same? Well, customers like to be treated differently, specially. They like you to use their language, not yours. They like prices that feel right. They like products that suit their particular needs. Bit it's not just about the customer: it's about you, too. It's about maximising productivity and profits for each market segment. It's about prioritising your efforts – selecting which segments are more important than others, which segments have more long-term value and which segments are simply dead ducks.

So how do you segment your market? Let's take an example. Imagine you run an electrical wiring and installation business called e-Lectric. You install and maintain power systems in houses, small offices and small shops. You could segment your market by customer type: consumers, businesses and shops. Your site could ask customers for a little information on the type of customer that they are ('Click here if you're a household'/'Click here if you run an office'/'Click here if you run a shop'). You could also segment your market by territory: north, south, east and west of the city ('Please enter your postcode'). Or you could segment by a budget: under £1,000, under £5,000 and over £5,000 ('Please select the services you require').

How to segment

There are many kinds of segmentation.

Geographic

This is simply where people live or where companies are based. You might choose postcodes or cities, or you might get a little more fancy and choose housing types in certain areas (e.g. four bedroom plus), or companies located in business parks, or in multiple-occupancy office blocks.

In e-Commerce, you can ask customers to submit their postcode, city or premises type when they register. Or, if you have no customer-registration process, you could segment from the homepage, with a choice of links such as:

- Our office is in a business park
- Our office is in an office block
- Our office is in our own building

Demographic

This is essentially segmentation on the basis of statistical information about the customer. For consumers, this may be age, gender, income or education. For businesses, this may be business activity, turnover, number of employees or years trading.

In e-Commerce, customers may be more suspicious about revealing demographic information. Consumers and businesses are often reluctant to reveal their income, or other sensitive information such as age or number of employees. Tread carefully here!

Lifestyle

Segmenting by lifestyle is a little more subtle – it's about the way people or businesses choose to live, work or regard themselves. For consumers this may be by family (single, married but no kids yet, married with young kids, adolescent kids, kids left home), or for businesses this may be ambitious companies, steady-state companies or companies in search of help.

In e-Commerce, segmentation by lifestyle is pretty easy when you offer customer profiling on your site. If you invite customers to register as users or members, you can ask them to self-select the stereotype that most closely fits the way they see themselves ('I would describe myself as 1. sporty, 2. fit, 3. so-so, 4. couch-potato').

Behaviour

This is perhaps the most Internet-friendly form of segmentation. Behavioural segmentation monitors what customers do when finding, choosing, buying and consuming your product or service – or those of your competitors. For consumers or businesses, this could be the number of products compared, the timing or frequency of purchase, the volume purchase or sensitivity to price.

In e-Commerce, you can easily track where your visitors go, which pages they visit, which products they tend to buy, the frequency of their visits, the referrals they make to other customers, their payment preferences and their satisfaction ratings. When you start to segment your market on the basis of visitor behaviour, you can target your pricing, promotional messages and products very accurately towards the most productive and profitable customer groups. This is one of the enormous advantages of Internet segmentation.

Why segment?

First, we segment to prioritise, which leads to focus and strategy. When you segment your market, you're not doing it for fun. You're doing it to choose the most important segments, to recognise their specific needs and to meet them with a nonstandard product or service. And failure to segment usually causes a dull product or service.

Second, we segment to identify new possible kinds of customer – to be creative in where, and to whom, we sell. You may run a flower business, selling to restaurants and hotels. You could also be selling to hospitals, railway stations, retail, weddings, funerals, television studios, sporting events.

Third, we segment to block sales cannibalisation – in other words, to create incremental sales, not merely create new customers by stealing old ones. Say you run an office security company, with 250 active customers in the Devonshire area, and you plan to launch a new service. You could focus on the Cornwall area for office security or target light-industrial premises in Devonshire, in order not to have existing customers merely reject your old service in favour of your new.

Fourth, we segment to help us design a better product or service. It's helpful to create stereotypes of your chosen segments and to get to know them well. For instance, let's say you run a CD store. Your segments may be under-15 rebel, under-15 conformer, 15–25, 25–35 and 35 plus. That's a bit dry. How about these:

- **Jenny** (15) hates her parents, already smokes, pierced tongue, in trouble at school, spends cash as soon as she has it, never owns a CD longer than six months, spends £12 per week on music (CDs or gigs)
- **Chris** (14) studies hard, Arsenal fan, a bit spotty, collects CDs and never sells, saves his pocket money, works weekends, helps around the house, spends £12 per three weeks on CDs
- **Donald** (19), cool, *NME* reader, regular gig-goer, listens to XFM and Radio 1, works in design studio, lives at home still, reasonable disposable income, spends £20 per week on CDs

And so on. You might even put photos of them on your marketing office wall, just to get to know them better.

When you prepare your segmentation, here's a checklist, to make sure each segment is genuine, and doesn't overlap:

Segment checklist

All your segments should be D-FARM. That is, Distinctive, Future-proof, Attractive, Reachable and Measurable.

Is it distinctive? Not only in terms of its characteristics (e.g. age group, family income, number of employees) but also in terms of its boundaries (e.g., UK only, no kids in the family yet, in financial services). You really have to ask yourself a question here – is Segment A noticeably different from Segment B, or should I treat them as the same? For 'e-Lectric', an electrical fitter, high-street retailers in Birmingham and Manchester may be different in location, but may be no different in any other way.

Is it looking good in the future? Look 3–5 years ahead for a forecast – is this segment set to shrink? Is it set to become poorer? You need the segment to allow you to get a return back on your investment. For e-Lectric, the retailer segment may well be in decline.

Is it attractive to us? Look for segments that are good for profits, not oppressively competitive, well suited to your assets and capabilities. For e-Lectric, large houses with swimming pools may appear at first sight to be a lucrative segment, but the degree of specialist electrical work required may make it very hard to serve.

Is it reachable? This includes delivery and communications. If it's too expensive or impractical to serve or promote your business to a particular segment, then it's unreachable. For example, e-Lectric may wish to segment its office buyers according to their approach to negotiating. There may well be democratic, autocratic, deal-minded or pragmatic buyers in their market, but how will they identify which buyers fall into which segment? These are not really reachable segments.

Is it measurable? If you can't measure your market segment, how can you tell its size, its worth to you as a business – or compare it with other segments?

Is your focus in the right place? Online, you can segment by customer behaviour – which pages they visit, how long they stay, what they download, which button they push, what feedback or interests they reveal to you.

Segment selection

Now you've identified your true market segments, you need to select the high-priority ones. Let's say you started with four segments – A, B, C and D. You ruled out C during your 'D-FARM' exercise and you've got it down to A, B and D. You need to ask yourself, Which segments should I prioritise? These are the ones that score highest on both your capabilities and long-term importance (marked in grey).

Suitability of the segment to your assets and competencies

		High	Medium	Low
	High	A	B	
	Medium			D
	Low			

Profit or strategic importance of segment

Here, we can see that, out of four segments, the order of importance is A, then B. C and D are nonrunners.

Horizontal and vertical segments

Online, there are two types of segment – horizontal and vertical. They behave in different ways and have different and very important commercial characteristics. It pays to take heed of these.

Horizontal segments

The horizontal segment is a group of individuals or businesses who share common circumstances, such as where they live, how much they earn, age, education, gender or business activity, turnover or number of employees. These are known as demographics. There's usually very little customers can do about their demographics – they're there by circumstance more than choice.

By nature, horizontal segments, or online communities, are large and broad (almost horizontal you might say). But don't expect members of a horizontal community to feel as if they belong. Do you feel that you really belong to a special group of people with the same age as you? The same job as you? It's unlikely. However, if you go to a well-focused site that serves just graduates, or just entrepreneurs, you're likely to relate very strongly to the products or services available.

In other words, horizontal communities are generally less engaged in their community, and more engaged in product, site or brand.

Vertical segments

The vertical segment is a group of individuals who share common interests, passions or obsessions. For consumers this may be fishing, football or fashion. For businesses this may be team development, directors' responsibilities or customer service. There's usually a strong element of personal choice about vertical interests – they're there by choice, rather than circumstance.

By nature, vertical communities are narrow and compact (vertical, you might think) and much smaller than horizontal communities. They're very keen on learning from each other, sharing ideas and views. They have a sense of belonging. If you're passionate about four-wheel-drive jeeps, would you join a 4WD community? Very likely. If you're burning with passion about customer service, would you join a like-minded community? Almost certainly. But would you feel so excited about 4WD the brand? Customer Service Ltd, the company? It's unlikely (unless of course they were means to getting access to the communities).

In other words, vertical communities are generally much more engaged in themselves than they are in brand, product or site. So as entrepreneurs, how should we commercially exploit these differing communities?

	Horizontal Community	Vertical Community
Loyal to You	Harvest for sales	Encourage purchase of your product/service
Loyal to themselves	Encourage membership of vertical communities	Harvest for ideas

Getting the mix right

The trick is to get the mix of horizontal and vertical communities right. Get the verticals to create the buzz and the ideas. Get the horizontals to buy. And get them both to cross over! You'll probably need to encourage several vertical communities to broaden your site sufficiently to 'carry' the horizontal community.

Actually, this is easier than it sounds. Let's say you run a print brokerage, selling print services to businesses. Here's how you might approach your segment management:

	Horizontal Community = Print Buyers	Vertical Community = Digital Print Fans, Direct Marketers
Loyal to You	Harvest for sales	Create special digital print shop on the site. Create direct marketing print service

	Horizontal Community = Print Buyers	Vertical Community = Digital Print Fans, Direct Marketers
Loyal to themselves	Encourage print buyers to join a learning zone on the site with commercial hints and tips	Harvest both communities for new product ideas

Influence is a one-way process

When I meet e-Commerce clients for the first time, many of them explain their passion for the customer. The customer comes first, they say. The customer drives our business. We focus on customer service. I say, 'Prove it.' There's usually a long waffle about attitude or approach, which means very little.

But customer focus is most simply achieved by influence – allowing the customer to influence you. And this is most clearly demonstrated by five steps:

- ☐ Telling customers that you listen and when you will next listen to them (set a date for a meeting or event or a deadline for online feedback)
- ☐ Listening passively, without responding in a listening programme (described in Chapter 8)
- ☐ Deciding which suggestions are profitable and which pack competitive punch
- ☐ Putting the suggestions into practice in an innovation programme (described in Chapter 12)
- ☐ Telling customers that you've responded to their suggestions

Now think about your own company. Do you do any of these? Most companies don't. Most companies say they listen carefully, innovate frequently. And you may have the most creative team in the world, knocking out innovation after innovation. But that's not customer focus. That's just change for its own sake.

Ironically, the telltales signs are in the means, not the end. If you believe in the customer, you'll have a feedback system or programme that you can show others, not just hold in your head. If your business has a commitment to innovation, you'll have a decent system, which has a life or a diary of its own.

As an entrepreneur or a manager, *you* take the responsibility to make these things real. And one of the most effective ways of doing this is to tie your listening and innovation into segmentation. Say you run a haulier's firm, specialising in frozen goods. Here's how you might approach your listening and innovation:

	Frozen food to retailers segment	Frozen medicines to laboratories segment	Frozen ingredients to manufacturers segment
Telling customers you listen	Single suggestion box on every dispatch note which is signed by retailer	Combined quality and service focus-group every quarter	3-question telephone survey every quarter
Listening passively	Postcards to say thank you for suggestion	Letter or email from MD thanking customer for suggestions	Postcards to say thank you for suggestion
Choosing profitable or competitive ideas	Quarterly drivers meeting with managers, followed by marketing & financial analysis	Quarterly marketing and financial analysis	Quarterly drivers meeting with managers, followed by marketing & financial analysis
Making the Innovation	Sensitive quarterly briefing of drivers and warehousers	Sensitive quarterly briefing of drivers and warehousers	Sensitive quarterly briefing of drivers and warehousers
Telling customers about the customer-led improvement	Flyer to retailers, describing change and rates	Letter to customer, describing changes and rates	Letter to customer, describing changes, plus new rate card

Survey ten competitor sites

Take a close look at your competitors' sites. We are looking for ideas, for signs of competitive advantage and capabilities that are better than ours. We're looking for qualitative information, not statistics. The very worst we can do here is to match their functionality and the quality of their design, and the best we can do is to adapt their ideas, evolve them into something bigger and better, and launch them on our own site. Of course, we will be adding our own ideas and competitive advantages too. Here's a five-step list to guide you through qualitative competitor analysis:

1   Explore the whole site quickly, just as a customer would. Most visitors go straight to services or the e-Commerce part of the site – the meaty part. If you're already familiar with the site, sit down with a colleague who isn't, and discuss and record his views as he surfs. Which bits did you like best? Which bits stood out the most? What overall impression did you get? So what overall impression would you like to create with your site? Which bits are worth borrowing? Which bits are worth adapting?

2   Take a closer look at their homepage. Make a list of every single feature and function there. This might include navigation, pictures, shortcuts to important parts of the site, a welcome message, audience segmentation, a special promotion, animation, customer log-in, logo, search, a banner advert or internal advert, a customised 'my page' or some other specialist feature. Now ask yourself which features ought to be on your site. Which features impressed you, or conveyed something impressive? Which features implied professionalism, imagination, leadership, or value?

3   Register as a customer on their site, if you can. Again, record every single feature and function during the registration process. What information did they ask for? Did they ask for too much? What do you think they will do with the information? What could they do? Should you ask for less or more information? Now that you've logged in, which areas do you have access to that the public do not? Are these areas more impressive or less impressive than the public areas? Were you delighted or disappointed once you had logged in? What lessons can you learn from this registration process?

4   Make a purchase, without actually parting with your money. How easy was it to choose? Were you able to compare one product with another? Was it fun? Was the ordering process simple and intuitive? Which parts of the process would you like to borrow or adapt? Which parts could you easily do better in? Did you feel that you were visiting a secure, trustworthy site?

5   Finally, pop back and revisit the entire site quickly. This time, look carefully at their visual design. Check the colour scheme, the use of typography, the integration of photography and other

LITTLE e, BIG COMMERCE

images, the use of space. Is it appealing? Does it convey the company's character, give you an impression of what they're like as a group of people? How different will you have to make your site, so that customers can see the difference at a glance?

You should try to ignore the technical performance of the site during this process. If the site runs slowly or if certain pages cannot be accessed, do not let that distract you from assessing the quality of the functionality and design of the site.

Spy on competitor businesses

Now that you have had a good look at their sites, try to take a close look at their businesses. Most of us think this is harder than it really is. There are plenty of sources of competitor information which are readily to hand:

- Annual reports, public accounting records, credit reports, trade press, brochures, promotional literature and, of course, their website!

- Prices, distribution arrangements, advertising, promotions, proposal documents, introduction letters and of course email newsletters and press releases on their website.

- Conversations with suppliers, ex-employees, ex-clients and distributors.

- Anecdotal information from your own sales team, telesales team, account-management or customer-service people.

But what is it that we need to know? What information will reveal critical weaknesses that we can attack or strengths that we should be aware of?

	Quantitative	Qualitative
Easy to Get	• Sales • Profit • Market share	• Company structure • Sales structure • Web structure • Reputation and customer feedback
Hard to Get	• Sales by product • Sales efficiency • Web targets • Online sales • Territories sold to	• Customer retention • Quality of database • Service levels • Web services for customers only • Future plans

What are we going to do with this information? Indeed, why should we gather or even worry about it? Some companies prefer to ignore the competition. They like to focus on their own plans and their own style. Others become obsessive about competitors, and sometimes forget about their own vision. Of course, the best approach is a balanced one. The only reason you should track your competitors is because they represent the standard you must beat.

So what?

You've developed a clear picture of customers. You've segmented them sensibly, in a way that suits your working style – and that suits profit, too. And you've also taken a qualitative look at competitors, comparing yourself and projecting your competitive standpoint.

Chapter checklist

Do I have the following?

- A clear and prioritised definition of my market segments
- A mapping of horizontal and vertical communities
- A 5-step customer influence process
- A list of competitor functionalities that you need to beat

CHAPTER SIX

Set marketing strategies and targets

Strategy is simply how you do something. Initially, your e-Commerce strategy is about how you'll move existing commerce online. After that, e-marketing strategies apply.

I'm sometimes asked, 'Are there strategies that exist only in the digital world?' There are some, but not many. Most business and marketing strategies are common to both the offline and online worlds. But the online versions have a slightly different flavour, and so, while there's really nothing new here, they need thinking about in slightly different ways – and usually in less revered terms. In my experience, tactics and implementation matter as much, if not more, on the Internet as in the conventional world.

That's because, in the online world, it's generally less expensive and quicker to adapt or change course. So everyone does. And that makes change more important. In the offline world, mistakes in advertising, design, print and PR can be much more costly to fix. Get the strategy wrong and the cost of replacing tactical investment is high.

But this is no excuse for not having a strategy in the first place! An e-business can be just as rudderless and unsuccessful as a normal one!

Take five deep breaths before diving in

If you're new to the idea of e-Commerce, it is a good idea to steep yourself in its reality before diving into strategy. If you're not new to the idea, only to its implementation, it would be no bad thing to do the same. So take five deep breaths:

Breath 1: Take the Internet seriously

- [ ] Read the latest statistics: www.fletch.co.uk.
- [ ] Visit your competitors' sites.
- [ ] Visit award-winning sites. Daily list at www.yahoo.co.uk.

Breath 2: Read up quickly

- [ ] Read several books – not just this one. A list appears in the reference section.
- [ ] Read back-copies of a few magazines. *Internet Works* is good for practical hints and case studies, *Internet Business* for strategy.

Breath 3: Listen to staff who strongly advocate e-Commerce
Don't talk, just listen. Invite three staff for beer and sandwiches and ask for the full fire-and-brimstone sermon. Ask for the jargon-free version. Keep asking why, and keep asking about the benefits.

Breath 4: Listen to five online customers over lunch or a beer
Again, don't talk, just listen. Invite them out for lunch and ask them how they use the Internet for business:

- [ ] Research
- [ ] Competitor analysis
- [ ] Customer analysis
- [ ] Purchasing
- [ ] Selling
- [ ] Fun
- [ ] Family or personal

Ask them for their favourite sites and why they like them.

Breath 5: Create a calm voice of reason in your head
Don't get shaken by what you find. You may be about to embark on major change, but every decision needs to deliver benefits to customers

and profit to the company, and needs to feel right. Keep this little voice with you at all times during the coming months!

Now you've taken your deep breaths, you're ready to dive in to strategy.

Strategies for offline businesses

First, we're going to look at how to move an existing offline business online. Four main strategies come into play here.

1: Protect your existing custom

When you move online, some customers will follow. But others will remain ardent fans of the phone and fax. They'll still expect your commitment to conventional commerce.

It's your job to see that you protect this business. Hard-won customers are costly to lose. So a protection programme is wise. This might include:

- ☐ Dual promotions for offline and online business (e.g. 15 per cent off Product A for phone orders, 15 per cent off Product B for web orders)
- ☐ Blow-softeners (online prices for existing offline customers for three months)
- ☐ Improved delivery to offline customers, using online delivery partner
- ☐ Improved phone answering – more polite and swift than before
- ☐ Setting up telesales hotline ordering, basing their order system on the new website
- ☐ Publish the telesales hotline on website and literature
- ☐ Neutral policy among sales team on online/offline sales

Offline customers can be worried that their relationships with you will dissolve, or that their choices will be limited, or that they'll wind up doing more work for an order. Reassure them that it's OK to trade offline. That people are what drives your business, not software. Anyway, why should you dictate which medium customers use? Let them choose, and they'll be happier.

In fact it is a common mistake among many Internet start-ups to ignore the phone or physical meeting as a means of transacting business. Giants like Dell have consistently encouraged phone ordering from their printed literature and their website itself.

2: Beware of new markets

When you launch your new e-Commerce site, it's worldwide whether you like it or not. New markets that you couldn't previously reach will now be able to order direct. Even if you're not specifically targeting them, they may find you, even in small numbers. The tendency with first-time e-Commerce is merely to publish a new site. The focus goes on the site, not the service, not the customer. So how do you avoid this problem? How do you focus on serving?

Let's say you're a Glasgow-based travel agency, serving Glasgow holidaymakers. When you move online, now your marketplace expands to the UK. You'll need to serve your new market with quick email response, call-backs and next-day ticket delivery. You'll need to pay more attention to your customer's departure airport when handling sales enquiries. You can't assume the customer can drop in to pick up tickets or browse through your paper brochures – you'll need to put that side of the business online too. You may have to strike up partnerships with other travel agencies in the UK to handle local customers locally – especially the offline ones. This would mean networking with competitors!

If you can't or won't stretch to serve new (usually geographic) markets, then say so clearly on site. It's better to disappoint early than build up expectations and then dash them harshly, causing bad word of mouth.

Ensuring high levels of service and delivery are key to entering new markets online. Be prepared in advance, not after you lose your first hundred online disappointed customers!

3: Obey the fickle customer

In the offline world, you may enjoy rather more customer tolerance than you are aware of. Perhaps you have telesales or field sales staff who are good at persuading. Perhaps your order takers are expert at softening the blow of two-week delivery cycles. Maybe your production people are great relationship managers and can sweet-talk the customer into smaller batches, lower spec or later delivery. That just doesn't work online. The persuasive devices are absent. Your promise is visible and only one click away from your competitor's.

So tighten up and perform. You'll need to be much more professional in almost every area of your business when you move online. In many respects, commerce is simpler, more direct, more old-fashioned on the Internet. You promise, you deliver. That's your only option – because the e-customer has more buying power, more mobility and less loyalty, all conveniently supplied by the Internet.

4: Amplify everything that you're known to be good for

You have an existing reputation to protect. Your customers and your staff already have faith in that reputation. And that's an asset, a starting point for your differentiation on the Internet. If you were known for friendly service, illustrate on the site how your friendliness translates into customer benefits, perhaps using case studies. But don't just stop there. Make sure your staff are well trained in helping e-customers in a friendly manner who have queries or problems with using your site. Lock up your staff systems with your customer website, so staff can interact with customer orders on a live basis.

Sometimes, it's helpful to think of your website as a caricature of your business. The site has all the look and feel of your company, but perhaps it's a little more engaging, a little more simplistic and hopefully a little more light-hearted!

Getting out of the starting gate

Now ask yourself a question: Do we pursue any of these strategies, even slightly, right now? Is this kind of approach to business even vaguely familiar to us? If so, where is the evidence?

Sadly, most small to medium-sized businesses – and some larger ones too – have no customer-retention programme, are inadequate to average service levels, have little customer focus and no reputation for being 'best in class'. And you may be the exception to the rule. But, when they start an e-Commerce project, many such businesses need a serious tune-up project at the same time. That's two projects and double the workload. Not surprisingly, many first-time e-Commerce projects fail.

So how likely is it that you'll be able to enact these strategies? Well, now you're aware, you can prepare. You can set up four mini-projects (one for each strategy) as a part of the main e-Commerce project. You can also adapt some of the start-up strategies on the next few pages – they're generally suited to existing offline businesses, too. Also, have a look at the build section in Chapter 10 on how to schedule these projects.

Strategies for new Internet businesses

Now let's examine the Internet start-up. You're designing a new business on the basis of an idea. You're probably blasting down ideas on paper, brainstorming features and thinking about customer behaviour. What are your main strategic options for this business?

You should consider the effect of functionality on your markets, and the degree to which they're likely to want to exert influence on you. Meaning what, precisely?

Well, if you're selling crockery to the wealthy over-thirties market, you may already have an idea to focus very narrowly on crockery alone, and avoid broadening the product range to cutlery, ovenware and so on. You may also be keen to move away from traditional designs towards more innovative and modern patterns. And let's say that your research shows your target customer wants to be able to design their own patterns, possibly even trade their designs on the market. What sort of approach is best? A choice of strategies would help to define the way.

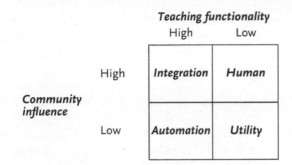

Utility strategy

This is all about making simple offers to uniform markets. Typically a low-budget operation, this is a strategy many businesses start with and find hard to sustain. It's well suited to businesses that provide self-selling or familiar products to broad uniform markets, such as retailers of food and videos or publishers of business information.

The strategy directs your business to adopt a no-frills approach to the site and customer service. It assumes your customer is happy to take things pretty much as they are, and that their loyalty is based on convenience and simplicity rather than depth and functionality.

Automation strategy

This strategy pushes high content and functionality to larger and less communicative audiences. The resulting sites are usually more expensive and take longer to build. The strategy is appropriate to companies that offer complex products, services or product ranges, which may require a lot of time in configuring or choosing. This would include computer equipment, stockbroking and recruitment.

The strategy directs your business to develop a comprehensive site, and to favour automated processes over human ones.

Human strategy

When you implement a human strategy, you're delivering a convenient and simple website to underpin a large offline operation. The site may be small or large, but it is still critical to the transaction of business. Indeed the customer may spend only a small amount of time online before engaging the human side of the business. This kind of strategy is suited to businesses that custom-make or repackage the goods or services of suppliers. It's also suited to those with high price tags, such as car sales, business consultancy, property sales and legal services.

The strategy directs your business towards an economical site, and to favour human processes in customer service.

Integration strategy

This appears to be the most ambitious strategy, yet it doesn't have to be expensive and is often very effective. The resulting sites are often customer-focused and engaging, resulting in high loyalty and a real buzz. The strategy is suited to businesses that sell information-rich products, connect customers to suppliers or combine tailorable products with trust. This would include online financial management, business travel and royalty-free picture-library services.

The strategy tends to direct your business to combine a powerful site with comprehensive human service.

Strategies for developing e-marketing

After you've established e-Commerce sales, and you've proven to yourselves that it's a viable activity, it's time to consider online expansion. And that means business development. Here, more conventional strategies help to focus our thinking.

If you're familiar with marketing or business development, you'll probably know of Ansoff's famous strategic-options matrix. Ansoff broadly defined four strategies for our different situations.

The Ansoff Matrix

		Product or Service	
		Existing	New
Market	Existing	Market Penetration Strategy	Product Development Strategy
	New	Market Development Strategy	Diversify Strategy

He came up with this idea in 1957, and it's been in virtually every single marketing textbook ever since. I remember the first time I came across this matrix. At first glance I thought, it seems simple. Then, when I started to think about what the strategies really meant, I wanted more detail. And in many ways, Ansoff's matrix is useless without its interpreter – the marketing mix.

When strategies change, the marketing mix changes accordingly. I like to use this simple marketing-mix table. I use it for my own business and those of my clients. It gives you an indication of how the marketing mix changes from one strategy to another, how the focus shifts.

The table below is a general guide, not a set of rules. As every entrepreneur knows, winning is applying the ideas, making the most of reality. But it's helpful to have a starting point. For each strategy, the most important tactics (i.e. where the money and energy are concentrated) are highlighted in grey.

	Product	Price	Promotion	Place
Product Development	Quality	High or entry	Heavy	Restricted
Market Development	Adapt	Competitive	Competitive	Focused
Market Penetration	Hold	Aggressive	Heavy	Wide
Diversification	Quality	Opportunistic	Opportunistic	Restricted

In e-Commerce, it's broadly the same. Now if you have a number of products or services – a portfolio, as the suits would say – then you need to pop each product into the matrix. In other words, there's at least one marketing strategy per product. Let's take an example – CandleNova, a UK-based candle manufacturer, specialising in novelty dining candles:

Product or Service

		Existing	New
	Existing	UK Dinner-table Candles	UK Candle Holders
Market	New	German Dinner-table Candles	German Candle Holders

Market penetration is selling more candles to the same kinds of customers it the UK. In other words, becoming more dominant, more of a leader in the marketplace. They would probably rely on heavy promotion and special offers to increase their sales in the UK, and would ensure that delivery within 48 hours to anywhere in the UK was a guarantee. They may also invoke a competitive strategy from the next chapter to rattle their major competitors a little.

Market development is launching the same candles in Germany. If the German market already has mid-priced competitors, CandleNova can do one of several things: undercut, run price-based promotions such as 'buy 10 get 5 free' or go to premium pricing and promote itself as classy, 'high-style'. Either way, price is going to be critical for comparative online shoppers and promotion is going to be the key device to underpin the image and positioning.

Product development is launching a range of stylish candle holders into their existing UK market. This involves developing and launching a brand-new product, and telling everyone about it. So critical elements of the marketing mix are going to be product quality and product awareness promotion.

And finally, diversification – a high-risk strategy always – is selling the candle holders to Germany. It's an unproven product in an unknown market. They may also be seeking to withdraw obsolete or unpopular candles to free up production facilities.

What happens to e-tactics

While all these major marketing activities are going on, four other tactics must harmonise. These are the e-tactics. They're the four essential elements of the Internet delivery. Again, for each strategy, the most important tactics (i.e. where the money and energy are concentrated) are highlighted in grey.

	Functionality & Content	Customer Service	e-Promotion	Delivery
Product Development	Quality	High	Heavy	Comprehensive
Market Development	Adapt	Competitive	Competitive	Competitive
Market Penetration	Refresh	Comprehensive	Heavy	Matching
Diversification	Redesign	Cross-sell	Nil	Raise Price

When your business applies these complementary e-tactics to the marketing mix, timing is the key. For instance, if you're launching a new range of candle holders into the UK, it makes sense to design and build a site at the same time as the product. It helps the team-building effort to tie up the enthusiasm, and stay focused. Naturally, you'll need to heavily promote the new product. And, of course, the follow-through activities of customer service and physical delivery must be of a high standard too.

Similarly, when you're about to embark on a sustained programme of market penetration, raising the standards of customer service and constantly refreshing the site content are perhaps the most appropriate areas in which to concentrate your efforts. Sustaining the promotional programme and level-pegging your delivery standards would underpin this.

Select the right target

Setting realistic targets is important, and nowhere is it more tricky than on the web. I've seen countless business plans and project plans that are based on finger-in-the-wind figures. 'If we assume 0.5 per cent market share within 12 months and an exponential growth curve, then profits will be 33 per cent in our first year.' I like that one. This is even better: 'Basing our sales projections on strong business interest in our phenomenal product, we predict linear sales growth to £2m turnover by month 12.' Wow! And these aren't exaggerations. They're typical of many plans that arrive at our office. One thing you can assume in e-Commerce is that your assumptions are likely to be wrong unless tested. But get used to the idea of using cautious ones – you'll have to make assumptions to set targets and plan your resources.

So how do you set targets? Well, there are three important parts to targeting, assuming (no pun intended) you've done your research and are aware of both the opportunities and the threats out there in the marketplace.

- The size element. How ambitious are you? What feels challenging, but doable? This depends largely on how much risk you feel like taking, and how deep your pockets are.

- The aim element. Specifically, is it sales, customer growth or customer retention that we're after? Meaning, are we going for short-term, aggressive and probably investor-backed growth? Or are we going for more organic, longer-term, community-empowered trade? Or are we trying to retain, even grow, the customer base while we move our offline business online?

- The real-world element. The reality check that good revenue modelling can bring (there's a section on this in a few pages' time).

Now you may wish to combine two or all three of these. You may have different kinds of targets for different market segments. But they should always be centred on commercially valuable wording:

- Online sales or orders worth £X by Y date
- Online live customers worth £X by Y date
- Online repeat customers worth £X by Y date
- Online new customers worth £X by Y date
- Online vocal customers worth £X by Y date
- Online referrals worth £X by Y date

And, yes, you may have to make assumptions about the value of a customer. Be cautious. If you hope they'll make four purchases a year, assume two. If market research says customers spend an average of £250 a year on your kind of service, assume you get the ones with the £100 budgets.

Advertising targets

If you're running a site that's aimed at a wide audience, targeting very high volumes of daily traffic, you may have considered advertising revenue as an important part of your business model. Setting the right target in this instance means 'advertising hits' – probably the only time you'll ever need to measure hits, as opposed to page views.

To reinforce your targeting, you might like to contact the Audit Bureau of Circulation – Electronic (ABCE) at www.abce.org.uk or the Internet Advertising Bureau (IAB) at www.iab.net. They can give you stats on what traffic figures flow across major sites. Your interest here is in comparing traffic with promotional effort and the age of the site, to build a picture of what you might expect for your own site. You may get a nasty shock when you realise the scale of investment that goes into sites with large traffic volumes. Don't be put off, though – most of them started small.

You can of course, ask the ABCE or the IAB to audit your traffic – you'll probably need to if you're to gain the trust of advertisers. This is expensive and requires quite a bit of technical fiddling about on your part, so you may wish to pay for the service once a year. It's important to distinguish between measuring (your responsibility) and authenticating the method of measurement (the auditor's responsibility). You'll still have to do the measuring – and to the auditor's standards, not yours!

To get an ABCE certificate, you'll need to do the following:

☐ Join the ABCE
☐ Release your server and database logs to them for review
☐ Tweak your logging processes to comply with ABC guidelines
☐ Submit, say, a month's logs
☐ If you comply with the ABC guidelines, you get your certificate

The hit myth

Don't measure hits! Measure visitors, repeat visits, impulse purchases, sales. Use statistics that are meaningful to you, not a computer.

And how do you measure these meaningful stats? In what units? Where does the information come from? From the original source, the server log files. Boy, now we're getting technical. Every night, your web host organisation will have programmed its servers to compile a list of all the technical activity on your site. And, now it's Monday morning, you want a clear picture – graphs are ideal – of what's really been happening trafficwise.

You'll need a technical person to convert these files for you. And they'll need a brief from you – don't expect a propeller head to know or care about marketing! Or, if you're software-literate, you might try HitList, WebTrends or FunnelWeb, which offer traffic analysis programmes.

Before we dive into the meaning of the stats, let's make an important distinction. Server logs are generally best for stats on public access. And database logs are generally best for stats on customers.

Why? Because server logs record which pages were opened, when and by which session (note: session, not person!). But database logs can record which person viewed which page, and when. It can also record submissions to the site – such as buttons clicked, options taken, forms filled out and so on. The catch is, you can't easily make one log do the work of the other. So it's best to have two logs, and combine them.

Server log files

So what stats can you get from the log files?

☐ Number of user sessions (the total number of visits made by customers – assuming, say, fifteen or thirty minutes per visit)
☐ Number of password users (the total number of known customers who have visited – i.e. those who have a password to get into protected areas)

- [ ] Number of page views per web page (this is the popularity of every page on the site – obviously the homepage will score highest, but which pages do customers go to next most often?)
- [ ] Number of unique visitors to the site (this can never be more than an estimate because users are not recognised by the server – only their technical machine-to-machine ID)
- [ ] Number of page views (also an estimate if you have a database-driven site, or a frames-based site, because servers don't recognise many database page loads)
- [ ] Durations of user sessions (reliable estimations of the total duration of each visit – although the server cannot distinguish between a visitor who made a coffee in the middle of a single visit and a visitor who left the site and returned for a second visit within five minutes)
- [ ] Number of files downloaded (a variant of page views, but focusing on particular files that you may have made available for download)

Now if all that seems a little technical, let's convert it to English. You can analyse these figures using spreadsheets or specialist analysis software to deduce:

- [ ] Where visitors came from
- [ ] What paths they followed
- [ ] Which pages people spend more time on
- [ ] Which pages are unpopular enough to be removed
- [ ] Which search words people used to find you from search engines
- [ ] How your navigation system is being used
- [ ] Which links on your site no one ever clicks
- [ ] What happens when you change parts of your site

Database log files

Of course, you don't have to use just server logs. As a marketer, or a manager, you'll want more. You can conduct a proper, more detailed analysis of customer – not visitor – behaviour.

You can get your own database to spit out statistics. The advantages of using this is that you can ask for very unusual or tailored stats, and you can get more detailed information on transactions or data submitted by customers. These are generally registered users – the real asset of your e-Commerce programme.

So what stats can you get from a database log? Almost anything you like, provided you have a techie on hand to build the functionality for you.

- [ ] Customer profiles
- [ ] Purchase or order profiles
- [ ] Sales enquiry profiles
- [ ] Complaint profiles
- [ ] Response to online promotional effort
- [ ] Response to offline promotional effort

And I'm sure you could add more. The great strength of a database log is its ability to track exactly what you want.

So what?

You've overcome the strategy hurdle. You've prepared properly for the planning part of the project and developed a clear set of enterprise strategies, based on whether you're starting a new business or a new site for an old business.

Chapter checklist

Have I the following?

- [ ] Taken five deep breaths before considering strategy
- [ ] Either four strategies for getting my offline business online . . .
- [ ] . . . or one selected strategy for my Internet start-up business
- [ ] An e-marketing strategy for each product-market pair
- [ ] An outline of e-tactics
- [ ] A clear statement of our targets

CHAPTER SEVEN

Prepare competitive strategies too

Once you've set out a strategy for your business, you need to arm yourself with a few approaches to competitors.

What is a competitive digital strategy?

It's conventional competitive strategy set in an online environment. So there's no rocket science, no myth, nothing difficult about it, just the adaptation of normal competitive strategies. And what are those? you may be wondering. They're essentially ways of attacking competitors or defending your products over a period of about one to two years.

But, in digital strategy, the time frame is usually a little shorter, unless you're a market leader. There are really only ten competitive digital strategies. For the most part, they're based on military strategy for attacking or countering an enemy – the competitor. And if, like me, you're suspicious of anything borrowed from the military, just see how real they are when they are applied to e-business!

The ten competitive strategies

1 Full frontal attack
2 Flanking attack

3   Surround and cut off
4   Blocking attack
5   Guerrilla attack
6   Niche defence
7   Territorial defence
8   Mobile defence
9   Stealth defence
10 Diplomatic nous

These strategies are useful and appropriate in different ways and in different circumstances. Let's examine them in more detail.

1. Full frontal attack

This is all-out war. Expensive, risky, long-term and winner takes all. You need money, courage and a strong product or service proposition that probably can't be beaten but maybe can be matched. It's a war of focused attrition – you pick a fight with a particular competitor, and throw everything you have at them. Naturally, as you can't take your eye off your other business, this requires extra people and resources.

Online, you'll need a groundbreaking site to start with, and an enormous PR and promotional campaign to persuade customers of your superiority. When you deploy this strategy, you develop a reputation for aggression and leadership.

Full frontal attacks are less common than other strategies but are used in online industries where comparative marketing is common – such as computer hardware, cars, lawnmowers and telecoms.

2. Flanking attack

This is striking at an area where a competitor is already weak, and therefore less likely to respond aggressively. You need to attack quickly with your most powerful weapon (perhaps price, perhaps service, perhaps innovation), and achieve an early, conclusive victory. This attack is more economical than full frontal, but delivers smaller results.

Online, you may need a special area of your site dedicated to the attack. This is likely to be a special price offer, a new product or service, better technology or better delivery. If these are areas where your competitor is weak, then your campaign will have bite.

Flanking attacks are commonly used by online businesses attacking offline businesses; the competitor's weakness may simply be the absence of a decent (or any) website! But they are used successfully across many industries and typically among bigger and market-leading companies.

3. Surround and cut off

This strategy is simply about surrounding your competitor – or a particular product of theirs – with a variety of products, product features, or offers. You need to be very focused and innovative to pull this strategy off, and chances are that you'll be in a fairly mature market, with years of experience in creating innovative variants from a standard product. Like the frontal attack, this is a long-term war of attrition. You will need deep pockets and plenty of resources to successfully pull this one off.

Online, you'll need a highly advanced website to start with. You'll also need a highly segmented communications programme to target different segments with different messages and different benefits, thereby surrounding your competitor.

Surround and cut off is effectively used by portals and shopping malls against individual niche specialists. Portal customers are bombarded by choice, price or alternative products, while the customer of the niche specialist is bereft of options. It's a very effective strategy for larger businesses attacking smaller ones.

4. Blocking attack

In this strategy, you are seeking to close out your competitor from important market segments, channels, affiliates or distributors. And the way you achieve it is by broadening your product or service range to supply everything that the customer, channel, affiliate or distributor desires. In effect, you're turning yourself into a one-stop shop, not just for customers but also for intermediaries.

Online, you'll need to expand your product catalogue, broaden your services to channels or affiliates, increase your appeal to new market segments and quite possibly reposition your entire business as a one-stop shop.

Blocking attack is perhaps most effectively used by customer-led organisations, who are better skilled at listening to customers, identifying their needs and going straight into production to satisfy them. More production-focused organisations tend to hesitate at strange or unfamiliar requests, or grow cautious when confronted with the need to expand core competencies.

5. Guerrilla attack

Guerrillas are good at five things: surprise, speed, economy, flexibility and self-knowledge. Guerrilla strategy is about co-ordinating these strengths to your maximum advantage against a competitor, on a micro basis. Typically, this may involve a hostile PR campaign, issue-based marketing that generates widespread publicity, parasitic deals that convert competitor offers into currency on your own site, or highly localised aggressive attacks on super niche markets. The trick is to use your speed, surprise and flexibility to fight on your own ground – your own terms, rather than those of your competitors.

Online, you'll need a top-notch publicity machine and, probably, specialist areas on your site, which may exist for only a matter of months before being archived and replaced with the next guerrilla campaign. A strong customer community that is well-informed by your email program is likely to underpin this strategy.

Guerrilla attack is commonly used by smaller aggressive businesses and superb publicists. If you have neither of these two skills, you can acquire them quickly – and easily. Guerrilla attack often rescues small businesses from sales paralysis and larger businesses from mediocrity.

6. Niche defence

Niche strategy is about specialising – using highly advanced skills, or very specialised products or services. It's a perfect defence against larger competitors, but it's also a perfect attack against lazy or complacent competitors. At its heart, this strategy depends on a strong customer proposition. Many companies mistakenly believe that if they're small they must be niche; in fact it is *skill* that makes a niche specialist.

Online, you'll need a web name, design and superbly detailed functionality to demonstrate that you are a supreme specialist. You'll need a community that feeds its obsession both to you as a learning business, and to itself as a passionate market segment.

Niche defence is almost entirely used by highly skilled or highly specialised companies. Specialism provides a rich terrain for passionate, committed and loyal customer behaviour. It's also a great opportunity for premium pricing, and many nichers do charge higher prices.

7. Territorial defence

Territorial defence strategy involves concentrating your business on a single geographic or community-based part of a market segment. Effectively, you're saying to competitors, 'Don't even *think* about coming in here – we've got it sewn up.' This strategy depends on your ability to develop a superb local market or community knowledge, and is very similar in some respects to niche defence.

Online, you'll need to create a regional or community flavour in your site design and functionality. If your territory is regional, you'll need to underpin your site with phenomenal local delivery and service in the offline world. And, if your territory is community-based, you may need to underpin your site with broader services or products which deepen the appeal of your offering and the loyalty among your community.

Territorial defence is commonly used by smaller businesses with a geographic focus, or a specialist, community-based business or portal, such as suppliers to football fanzines, or cosmetics companies serving lipstick collectors, or toy stores serving model railway enthusiasts.

8. Mobile defence

This strategy is akin to permanent innovation. It involves keeping your business and your site constantly ahead of the competition. It's a tricky strategy to pursue if you're a mediocre business, but, if you've got a genuine reputation for the cutting edge, then staying ahead is already a natural part of your business.

Online, you'll need visual and functional evidence of your advanced approach – possibly a new-technology dominance and an email and publicity machine that is geared towards cranking out groundbreaking stories.

The mobile defence strategy is ideal for the avant-garde, the style gurus, rebellious businesses and red-hot innovators. Software companies, technology businesses and opinion-forming organisations often pursue this strategy. You'll be constantly reinventing yourself, and demonstrating leadership where others have copied, plagiarised or licensed your ideas.

9. Stealth defence

Stealth defence is an underground strategy, like the French Resistance in World War Two. The idea is to make yourself invisible to competitors and press and rely totally on word of mouth. It differs from guerrilla strategy in one key way: marketing, communications and delivery are all underground, silent and unannounced, whereas the guerrilla uses publicity as a main weapon.

Online, you'll need a site unpublished on search engines, largely password-protected, and a heavy reliance on email and discussion-forum communication. To complement the secrecy, you'll need experience in starting a word-of-mouth effect, knowing how to reach opinion formers and how to create strings of influence.

Stealth strategy is used by, among others, the entertainment, personal services and surveillance industries. It's an excellent way to create a buzz, without a large budget, and with an opportunity for premium pricing.

10. Diplomatic nous

Diplomatic-nous strategy is about using deals with third parties to create more commercial power. It's about outmanoeuvring your competitors – and collaborating with them! You need excellent negotiating skills to pull off this strategy, but it's so very effective in Internet marketing that it's worth a go.

Online, you're looking to create functional and content links (not just brand associations or hyperlinks) or to forge joint marketing programmes that may result in joint licensing, distribution, production, research or communication deals.

Commonly, diplomatic nous is used by innovative and enterprising smaller businesses looking to find fast routes to growth. Internet start-ups often seek licensing or distribution deals to get quick growth established early in the life of the business.

So where do these 10 strategies best apply? And where are they inappropriate? Let's consider a number of scenarios.

David v. Goliath

Approaches to attacking bigger competitors
The advantages you should hold over competitors:

> ■ Speed, flexibility, diplomatic nous

The advantages you may hold over competitors:

> ■ Innovation, specialism, self-knowledge, territorial advantage

The weaknesses you're likely to have:

> ■ Finance, resources, product range, economies of scale

The approaches you can take:

> ■ Flanking attack
> ■ Guerrilla attack
> ■ Niche defence
> ■ Territorial defence
> ■ Diplomatic nous

Special concerns for start-ups:

> ■ Establishing a brand name and audience awareness of your presence is hard and increasingly is becoming expensive online. The territorial defence is unlikely to work straight away, as community and loyalty must be built over time.

David v. David

Approaches to attacking equally small competitors
The advantages you should hold over competitors:

- No special advantages relative to your competitor

The advantages you may hold over competitors:

- Competitor knowledge, innovation, self-knowledge

The weaknesses you're likely to have:

- No special weaknesses relative to your competitor

The approaches you can take:

- Flanking attack
- Blocking attack
- Guerrilla attack
- Niche defence
- Territorial defence
- Diplomatic nous

Special concerns for start-ups:

- Being prepared for competitor innovation is almost impossible as a start-up. In the six or so months that it may take to go from idea to a live site, your competitor may have already trumped your business idea. Again, the territorial defence is unlikely to work straight away, as community and loyalty must be built over time.

Goliath v. David

Approaches to attacking smaller competitors
The advantages you should hold over competitors:

- Finance, resources, product range, economies of scale, market experience

The advantages you may hold over competitors:

> ■ Innovation, self-knowledge

The weaknesses you're likely to have:

> ■ Speed, flexibility, competitor knowledge

The approaches you can take:

> ■ Frontal attack
> ■ Flanking attack
> ■ Surround and cut off
> ■ Blocking attack
> ■ Diplomatic nous

Goliath v. Goliath

Approaches to attacking large equal competitors
The advantages you should hold over competitors:

> ■ No special advantages relative to your competitor

The advantages you may hold over competitors:

> ■ Innovation, market experience, product range

The weaknesses you're likely to have:

> ■ No special weaknesses relative to your competitor

The approaches you can take:

> ■ Frontal attack
> ■ Flanking attack
> ■ Surround and cut off
> ■ Blocking attack
> ■ Diplomatic nous

2nd mover advantage

How to arrive late in an e-Commerce market and still succeed
The advantages you should hold over competitors:

> ■ Understanding of competitor mistakes, better understanding of market and appropriate investment, competitor knowledge

The advantages you may hold over competitors:

> ■ Finance, resources, product range, market experience, flexibility

The weaknesses you're likely to have:

> ■ e-Commerce experience, all the easy customers are with competitors, speed (you're behind already)

The approaches you can take:

> ■ Blocking attack
> ■ Guerrilla attack
> ■ Niche defence
> ■ Territorial defence
> ■ Diplomatic nous

1st mover disadvantage

How to defend against copycat and late-entry better sites
The advantages you should hold over competitors:

> ■ e-Commerce experience, greater recognition of your brand, all the easy customers should be with you, speed (you're ahead already)

The advantages you may hold over competitors:

> ■ More experience of innovation or market, product range

The weaknesses you're likely to have:

> ■ No precedent to follow, more expensive market entry

The approaches you can take:

> ■ Flanking attack
> ■ Surround and cut off
> ■ Blocking attack
> ■ Guerrilla attack

- Niche defence
- Territorial defence
- Diplomatic nous

Low budget

Approaches to defence if you can't afford e-Commerce
The advantages you should hold over competitors:

- No special advantages relative to your competitor

The advantages you may hold over competitors:

- Innovation, market experience, product range

The weaknesses you're likely to have against competitors:

- Finance, resources, weakened reputation

The approaches you can take:

- Guerrilla attack, using only a brochure site
- Mobile defence, using only a brochure site
- Diplomatic nous, sourcing funds or functionality from third party

So what?

You've really started thinking about competition now. You've thought about your strategic position carefully, and weighed up all the possible competitive strategies. You've selected those most appropriate to your situation on the basis of informed choice.

Chapter checklist

Do I have the following?

- [ ] A clear understanding of my competitive position
- [ ] A good contingency strategy ready for defence
- [ ] A good attacking strategy for major competitors

CHAPTER EIGHT

Choose an online business model

Now you have good research and clear strategies, you should choose which business model is right for you. This involves understanding how they work, and more importantly, what their implications are for operations.

Select from the main e-Commerce models

As e-Commerce matures, a number of business models are becoming clear. An Internet business model is simply a schema for business processes that shows, broadly speaking, where the goods and the money flow. Here are the most common ones starting with the simplest.

Office model

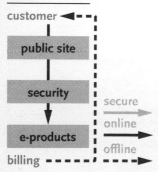

The Office model is essentially an extranet. An extranet is just a part of your website, which is visible only to clients. It's not visible to the public – or competitors. It's the cheapest business model on the Internet and is well suited to businesses making their first entry on to the Internet.

Best suited to

- service businesses
- high-value products
- collaborative projects or transactions
- services or markets with complex security arrangements

The limitations

- invoicing and payment are usually separate – higher manual costs

The Office model is one of the hardest to spot, because the most valuable part – the functional part – is often hidden by password protection. To first-timers, this is part of its appeal – the part of the site that the entrepreneur wishes to protect from prying competitor eyes is the part that can most easily be hidden.

Shop model

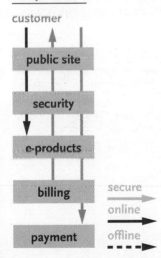

The shop model is the one with which we are most familiar. A catalogue lies at the heart of the site. Users search the catalogue, choose items from it, add them to their basket or shopping trolley and then move to the checkout area to pay.

Best suited to

- shippable or downloadable products
- low human intervention

The limitations

- can restrict service flexibility

Most of the world's largest online stores and most high-profile websites use this model. It's easy, familiar and predictable. Just what customers want. But it's also very public. Your competitors can easily copy what you may have spent months building. So it's a good idea to protect your site by creating unusual and higher-quality offline processes, such as customer service, delivery speed, telesales and cross-selling programmes.

Membership model

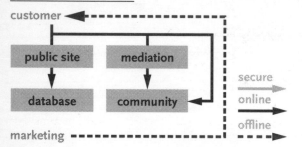

The membership model is all about creating a community that's of commercial value to your business. It's no good building a vibrant, buzzing community if you cannot generate financial returns from it. The key here is to plan your commercial activities before you create the membership system. Let's say that you run a business that supplies antique clocks. When you invite people to join as members, you might invite them to register for your weekly newsletter, which advertises, say, over fifty antique clocks for sale.

Best suited to

- sell-through of products or services
- customer communities

The limitations

- holes in community opinion

On the surface of it, the membership model offers no major e-Commerce opportunities. In reality, it is one of the most creative e-Commerce models, as it permits imaginative use of Internet communications. So it helps if you're a natural at PR, advertising, newsletters and special offers. It's also pretty cheap to produce a membership model site.

Market portal model

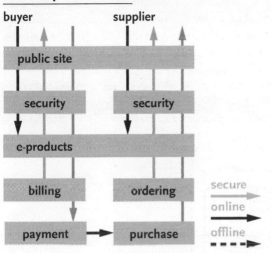

The market portal is one of the most recent models on the Internet. It's also one of the most aggressive. Outwardly, the market portal merely connects suppliers with buyers. But there's more to it than that. Successful market portals add value, by offering features or functions that make life easy for both buyers and suppliers. And that's why these two groups of customers will be willing to pay something to you, the site owner, as well as trading directly with the buyer or supplier.

Best suited to

- agencies or dealerships
- new Internet businesses

The limitations

- supplier participation

The interesting thing about market portals for small businesses or even for larger businesses making their first entry on to the Internet is that they are very aggressive. When you build a market portal, you can really cut out the middleman. In effect you become your own marketplace. You can quickly overtake many of your competitors by becoming the dominant source of goods or services in your market sector. This opportunity won't be around for long, though – as more and more Internet start-ups are filling the gaps in these markets. They have nothing to lose – they are not seeking to protect an existing customer base or any market share that they may have built up over years. They're looking for markets that may be like yours – so move quickly, or watch out!

You may have seen recently in the press a new breed of portal, called a 'vortal'. This is simply a vertical portal. In other words, a highly specialist portal marketplace, which is capable of solving almost any problem in just that one specialist niche. For example, 'building-materials-online' would be a portal; 'total-steel-solutions' would be a vortal.

Hybrids

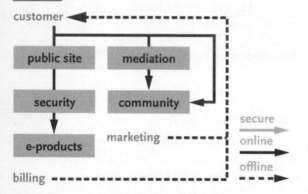

Most successful sites have a combination of parts of these models. Perhaps most frequently, the membership model is combined with one other. For instance, amazon.com is a membership and shop model combined. Buzzsaw.com is a membership and portal model combined. Have a look at your competitor sites and see how they've done it.

Learn from competitors and role-models

Most e-Commerce sites are based on the models described in the previous few pages. But adapting the model to your business is the key. The richest source of adaptation and implementation ideas for your site is of course on the Internet itself. Look at how others have done it. Knowing where to find these sites is easy. Here are a few dependable sources of information.

Learning from competitors' sites

This should be your first port of call. If you're not sure who your competitors are, ask your sales people (if you have any), look in the Yellow Pages, or use a search engine to generate a list. This is the nicest part of the research! You'll find out a lot about your competitors – their products and services, their marketing messages, their claims and competitive positioning. Of course, your competitors will be able to do just the same to you, once your site is live! Don't shy away from this – it often helps to be able to set out your stall publicly, to let your competitors know that you've staked a claim on the territory of, for instance, creativity, speed or a specialism in customers resident in Birmingham.

Learning from hot sites

Most major search engines compile a list of 'cool sites' which they spotted in the last week or so. They're usually listed on the basis of their design or their unusual specialism, and that's what makes them such useful model material. Good design and specialism are two positive components that you should consider weaving into your site.

Learning from staff

Ask your staff for their favourite sites. Ask them why they like them and, also, how they found out about them. Nine times out of ten, their favourite site will be rock-climbing, speed garage music or some other personal-interest site, but you'd be surprised how many useful and well-designed sites surface when you ask staff. That is, of course, if you have provided staff with Internet access at work! If you haven't, or don't intend to, think carefully here – if you're going to put the business online, generate enthusiasm for web working and increase your surveillance operation on competitors, how can you possibly do it without staff being on the Internet? (I often hear, 'I don't want my staff surfing all day on their favourite sites' to which I usually reply, 'OK, so you don't want to exploit valuable competitor information, to generate new ideas for your own site, keep track of the changes on the Internet, or find out what customers think.')

Learning from magazines

Another excellent source of information is the Internet magazine shelf in large newspaper shops. When you pick up magazines such as *Internet Works*, *Tornado Insider*, *Create Online*, *Computer Arts* or *Internet Business*, you'll find this month's specials – and you'll usually get some useful information on how they were put together, who built them and what the brief was.

Customer is king, queen, jack and ace

The best people to drive your website are your customers. It's important to make the distinction between decisions on content and decisions on implementation. Let your customers decide what content is best, and let your team decide how to implement those changes. It's just too easy to follow your instincts, to let the web team decide on new content, new functionality, new ideas. It's much harder to systematically check these ideas with – or to source them from – customers. So make a special effort to champion the customers' opinions at web team meetings. How?

Create a customer feedback system

Make it easy for your customers to provide qualitative and quantitative information. This usually involves one or more of the following:

- Customer feedback hyperlinks on the website, generating free-text qualitative emails to your web team or marketing team
- Customer feedback forms on the website, generating a combination of quantitative and qualitative comments on your products or services
- Customer rating forms on the website, generating simple scores for your products or services
- Discussion groups on the website, generating open discussion on your products or services
- Site-traffic analysis, generating statistics on which pages were visited most and how many visitors converted themselves to buyers

Create a twelve-week listening cycle

Listening is so important – it's worth drawing attention to it in a very public way. If you create a listening programme or a learning cycle, it sounds so much more active than just 'feedback'. And of course it gets staff to focus on customers. You can tie a listening programme up with your innovation cycle (*see* Chapter 12).

So whom should we listen to and what should we be listening out for?

- **Week 1** – Existing or live customers – feedback on service, quality, best and worst features and suggestions for improvement
- **Week 3** – Suppliers – feedback on pricing, competitor products, distribution and time scales to market
- **Week 5** – Prospective customers – feedback on needs, preferences, expectations

- [ ] **Week 7** – Partners/affiliates – feedback on promotions, pricing, market segmentation, reputation and product quality
- [ ] **Week 9** – Former customers – feedback on failures, successes, competitor products
- [ ] **Week 11** – Staff – feedback on promotion, success stories, failure stories, competitor success stories
- [ ] **Week 13** – Analyse the findings

Establishing this kind of programme is easy. Set up a simple feedback page on your site. Invite (or incentivise with prizes, a competition or other reward device) your targets to feed back, using the site. It takes one or two members of staff to chase the research and analyse the findings on a regular basis (say 2–3 days per month) and the management team to review the analysis and discuss them with staff.

Set up regular social events

Even if it's just beer and sandwiches once a month with your top ten customers or your affiliates, show that you listen. Try not to make these sessions too heavy-going – keep them light and humorous, but with the emphasis totally on listening. If you encounter criticism, don't try to put your point of view across. Listen carefully, acknowledge what your customer has said, and thank them. As soon as the lunch is over, write down all the feedback and pass it over to the web team, who should integrate the findings with the twelve-week listening cycle.

Value, not technology

Too many businesses make the mistake of focusing on technology rather than value, when they make their entry into e-Commerce. It's an unforgivable, big mistake, so don't make it! Customers don't buy your technology, your catalogue or your graphics. They buy value, so make sure you have it in spades!

Perhaps the most effective way of enshrining value at the heart of your e-Commerce programme is to link four simple systems to your website. If you set out these systems before your site goes live, then you have an excellent chance of delivering real value to your customers.

Service system

Most businesses aspire to high levels of service. They like to claim it in their brochures, claim it in their sales presentations, use it as a differentiator when explaining what makes them unique. But for most markets service is not a differentiator. Never has been. It's a must-have; it's what customers expect, and the lack of it is the one item most likely to drive away new customers. What makes good service on the Internet?

- [ ] Delivery on time
- [ ] Human beings to help
- [ ] Rapid response to email enquiries
- [ ] Compensation for mistakes or inadequacies
- [ ] Orders-status information
- [ ] There is a link between email enquiries and orders status and the website, to demonstrate to the customer that they have been heard and that you are acting on their behalf

If you can create a system that delivers at least three of these items, you're well on your way to good Internet service. Take a look at the Black Star videos site (www.blackstar.co.uk). You'll find four of these components making an excellent service system.

Customer relationship management

In my experience, very few businesses find customer relationship management (CRM) easy. Today most managers are aware that retaining customers is far cheaper than winning new customers. Yet surprisingly few of us seem to achieve effective relationships with our customers. This is probably because CRM differs from industry to industry. But there are some core common components to successful CRM:

- [ ] There is a regular review of each customer's account, which monitors finance, needs and the status of the relationship – each of these areas has actions
- [ ] Problems are never swept under the carpet – they go on to a problem list, from where they are solved
- [ ] There is a link between the relationship status of the individual customer, and the registration system of the website, so that the website can respond sensitively when the customer logs on
- [ ] All customer-facing staff are good communicators
- [ ] There is a single person who is responsible for each individual customer or a group of customers

Again, if you can create a system that delivers at least the first two of these, then you're well on your way to effective customer relationship management on the Internet.

Publishing system

A key part of successful e-Commerce is publishing – the business of constantly refreshing your site, with new and exciting copy and pictures. It's not difficult to be good at publishing – perhaps that's why it's often overlooked as an essential component. There's an easy way to keep publishing in mind – create a publishing system:

- Appoint one of your staff as the web editor, or subcontract this out to your web-design company
- Set dates in the diary – monthly as an absolute minimum – for the regular updating of the text and pictures on the site
- Harmonise the publishing system with the twelve-week innovation cycle
- Agree with the web team which parts of the site should remain static and which parts should be updated by the publishing system – ask yourself here what the customer would expect to see updated, and don't limit yourself to what is convenient to you
- Consider the following areas as a starting point for the dynamic content of your site: press releases, promotional offers, homepage headlines, customer feedback results, success stories, the catalogue, discussion forums, frequently asked questions (FAQ)
- Consider a weekly or monthly programme of email newsletters, which briefly describe your recent successes, new products and services and the results of customer feedback: always keep these as brief as possible and avoid any 'sales' exaggerations

If you can assemble at least two or three of these component parts within one programme, you're likely to generate positive feedback from customers and create a credible reason for their returning to your site on a regular basis. Try to add your own ideas and actions to beef up and customise the publishing system so that it's just right for your business and your customers.

Delivery system

Probably the biggest part of generating repeat business is delivery. Delivery is quite simply doing what you promise you will do. You could have the best site in the world and still fail to deliver. Through a large part of 2000, this is arguably what happened to Dell. A superb site – probably one of the best in the world – and yet still it took over three weeks for their products to be delivered. The laptop on which I wrote this book took nearly five weeks to arrive! Let's just say that Dell moved from being an exemplar in my mind (and in the seminars that I run, in the publications I write, and in the illustrations that I give to clients) to being a first-class model of how *not* to deliver!

For service businesses

Let's say you run a training business, specialising in management training. Your website is packed with useful content and functionality, and your service system, publishing system and customer relationship management system are all working brilliantly. What components might you put into your delivery system?

- Ordering – your site automatically confirms a booking when customers place an order
- Delegates' registration – a small form allowing you to register the names and email addresses of all delegates who will attend the training course
- Delegates' information – your site automatically emails all delegates with succinct details on the training course they are attending, the venue details, dress code, and a summary CV of their trainer
- Advance welcome notice – the day before a training course begins, your site automatically emails a warm brief message, saying how much the trainer is looking forward to working with you
- Training – at the opening and closing parts of the day, the trainer asks all delegates to provide feedback, and notifies everyone that they'll be getting an email
- Feedback email – the day after the training course ends, your site automatically emails a thank-you message which contains a unique link to a customer-satisfaction form on the website
- Feedback page – your site automatically captures very simple rating and feedback information, dumping the information straight into a database, so that the web team can easily analyse one month or one course's worth of information at a time

For product businesses

Let's say you manufacture beauty products for women. Your website is very popular and you have already successfully created systems for publishing, customer relationship management and service. What approach might you take to ensuring delivery is correct every time?

- Ordering – your site automatically confirms receipt of an order
- Order tracking – your site automatically emails a brief report, when the customer's order has been assembled and has been posted
- Payment – your site automatically confirms receipt of cash, together with a reassuring note that security on this site has never been breached
- Intranet – the staff who handle the order click the 'complete' button

CHOOSE AN ONLINE BUSINESS MODEL

after the order has been assembled and packed, and then again after it has been posted; this updates the database and drives the order-tracking functionality

- Feedback email – your site automatically generates an email to thank the customer for their business – the email contains a unique link to a customer-satisfaction page on the website

- Feedback page – your site automatically captures very simple rating and feedback information, dumping the information straight into a database, so that the web team can easily analyse one month's or one product's worth of information at a time

Delivery is so different from one business to another. Here we can see from these two examples how delivery depends on a combination of people and technology. When you sit down to devise your own delivery system, try to be not just imaginative, but as precise as you possibly can – the Devil's in the details!

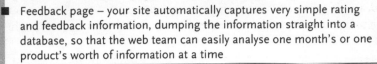

So what?

Now you're cooking. You've researched all the models, checked your market research, pencilled a twelve-week listening cycle and examined four systems to underpin value. Now you've done the hard thinking work, your business idea should be crystallising nicely. But what exactly is all this research and thinking good for?

Clarifying the business, of course. Ruling out unsuitable options. Eliminating doubt. And creating your e-Commerce vision.

Chapter checklist

Do I have the following?

- [ ] An e-Commerce model that suits my business
- [ ] List of competitor and exemplar sites to analyse
- [ ] A first-draft twelve-week Innovation programme
- [ ] A first-draft customer-feedback programme
- [ ] A first-draft service system
- [ ] A first-draft publishing system
- [ ] A first-draft Customer Relationship Management outline
- [ ] A first-draft delivery system

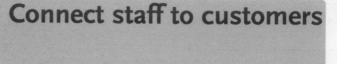

CHAPTER NINE

Connect staff to customers

This is your biggest chance to shine. Most online businesses – including start-ups – fail spectacularly at this fence. When all about you is a sea of mediocrity, it's not hard to shine!

Connecting staff to customers is probably the lowest-investment, highest-return activity that you can embark on in your e-Commerce project!

Not convinced? About four or five Internet start-up plans land on my desk every month. They are from entrepreneurs who have spent weeks, maybe months, fine-tuning a business idea upon which they are about to gamble their future and their reputation. These are companies that have pretty much all the time in the world to get it right – they are not under the kind of constant pressure that trading businesses experience. And do they contain imaginative recruitment and management systems? Do they embrace customer service in tangible, well-defined and well-staffed processes? Do they demonstrate how staff will build relations with customers right from the outset? Do they display an inkling of the human touch in their hi-tech world? Rarely. I've yet to see a start-up plan that maps out customer service as a key component of business success!

The alluring promise of the Internet – generating online sales with only the minimum of human interaction – somehow hypnotises even the most rational-minded entrepreneur. Be warned! The Internet is not an excuse to throw away your commercial sanity, and pretend that customers don't want relationships. They do! Not only that, they want to believe that your organisation is an organisation – not just a website!

So how do we go about the human side of e-Commerce? How do we put a human face to our digital interface? How do we add personality to online customer service? Well, we employ modern versions of a lot of old-fashioned, proven, relationship-building activities.

But, before we dive into these activities, let's look at the tools that your staff and customers will be using – intranets and extranets.

What is an intranet?

An intranet is the use of Internet technology *inside* a company. Your staff share customer and operational information and tasks. No one outside the company can see the intranet – it's protected by security.

How is it different from the Internet?

First, an intranet is a private network within your business, whereas the Internet is a worldwide, public network. Second, your intranet should have access to the Internet but not vice versa. Third, it's usually much faster, and therefore more suited to high picture content. And finally, because it's staff-only, you can train staff to use shortcuts and the kinds of tricky functions that you couldn't get away with on the public Internet.

How is an intranet different from our network?

It's as flexible as you need it to be. You can glue together old databases, share information among all staff that was previously available to only a few, or add new programs as you go along.

You can easily integrate programs such as email, calendars, Microsoft Office documents, templates, databases and presentations.

It's cheaper because it uses free browsers as the viewing tool – you don't need to pay for an expensive user licence for every head in the company. Of course, browsers run on PCs, Macs, Unix and other systems, so, if you have a mixed-computer office, the browser is close to ideal. As a single interface to a variety of information sources, the browser is also highly efficient and very easy to use.

You can find more information on the technical and practical aspects of intranets at www.intrack.com/intranet and http://navigators.com/intranet.html

The benefits of intranets

When used intelligently, intranets provide many benefits:

- [ ] help to cut software costs
- [ ] integrate previously unlinkable computer systems
- [ ] increase accessibility of information to all staff, not just a few
- [ ] improve customer relationships by improving customer management
- [ ] increase staff productivity by eliminating duplicate processes
- [ ] reduce errors by reducing manual tasks

What is an extranet?

It's the use of Internet technology outside a company's premises to share commercial and operational information and tasks with customers. No one outside the permitted customer group can see the extranet – it's protected by security.

How is it different from the Internet?

First, an extranet is a private network outside your business, whereas the Internet is a worldwide, public network. Second, your extranet should bar all unauthorised users. Third, you have complete control over what customers can and cannot see, and can legitimately monitor – and charge for – their activities. And finally, because it's customer-only, you can specify certain technology standards and train customers to use them, in a way that you can't do with the public Internet.

How is an extranet different from our website?

It's private. It's designed to deliver one-to-one information on a private basis to your customers. Confidential information such as finances, trading or ordering information, stock levels or contact details can be published on a secure basis. Also, important functionality can be offered, such as ordering, specifying, feedback and so on.

It's cheaper because, like an intranet, it uses free browsers as the viewing tool – you don't need to pay for an expensive user licence for every customer, or go installing – or supporting – software on their computers. And, if your customers have PCs, Macs, Unix or other systems, the browser is ideal.

The benefits of extranets

When used intelligently, extranets provide many benefits:

- [ ] help to cut customer software costs
- [ ] increase accessibility of information to customers

- [ ] improve customer relationships by improving their communications with your staff
- [ ] increase productivity by letting customers undertake certain processes
- [ ] reduce errors by reducing manual tasks such as order taking
- [ ] increase customer loyalty, by offering more frequent opportunities for engaging in or tracking your services

Connect staff to customers and customers to staff

This is the litmus test. You want to be an online business. You want to improve the way you work. You want to become a modern company. You want motivated staff, and dependable technology delivering excellent service to happy customers. You want high productivity, decent levels of automation and phenomenal management information. You want a well-informed management team, taking inspired decisions at breathtaking speed. Oh, and you have a tiny budget and your staff are too busy to deal with customers.

Wake up. If you really want to become an online business, you should really have a serious commitment to staff and customer systems.

Where are you going with customer service?

Are you taking sales orders, or satisfying customers? There's a huge difference. Are you committed to developing customer relationships, or to merely being polite on the phone? Do you expect your website to provide customer service?

You can't establish good customer service by technology alone. Some entrepreneurs think that 'customer relationship management' (CRM) is a database! Ever stopped to think about those words, and the order in which they appear?

1 Customer
2 Relationship
3 Management

When you're developing CRM, it helps to prioritise your efforts in that order. In other words:

- [ ] Customers first – what do they want? What are they saying? What are they not saying? Analyse their views.
- [ ] Relationship second – build a programme of activities for each customer or customer type, which will create the right conditions for a relationship – regular meetings, regular calls, regular emails, regular feedback, regular letters or regular customer events.

> ☐ Management third – do manage the customer, but don't let them feel as if they're being managed. Let them feel in control.

Remember, when all about you is a sea of mediocrity, all you need to do is raise your customer service 10 per cent higher than your strongest online competitor, and you're the leader.

How will you get there?

By combining people with technology to generate actions (the oldest goal of the modern age). And how do you do that? Share information (the oldest maxim of the Internet age).

These huge but very simple approaches break down into a number of smaller, more manageable chunks:

> ☐ Agree with sales and operations/production a simple set of critical events, such as enquire, order, adjust order, cancel order, confirm, pay, receive goods, feed back, complain, phone, email and meet
>
> ☐ Agree with the same staff what actions they will take at each event, and what technology they will change
>
> ☐ Set up your intranet so staff can monitor these activities – that is, see what customers are doing
>
> ☐ Set up the intranet and extranet to permit and monitor habits (regular click paths, products, order size, etc.) and preferences (stated choices, favourites, prejudices and settings)
>
> ☐ Set up your extranet so customers can do these things, and get your response – that is, transact and see what you're doing
>
> ☐ Train your staff to respond to these events, habits and preferences in a friendly and helpful way
>
> ☐ Create a related set of offline actions, such as letters, calls, meetings and events

What will stand in your way?

Ask yourself, 'What will stop us from consistently achieving excellent customer service?' Answer the question as truthfully and dispassionately as possible. It may be one or more of the following:

Problem	Solution
Budget	Work in phases
Existing workload	Work in phases, hire temporary staff
Technical skills	Recruit, subcontract or hire temporary staff

Problem	Solution
Management skills	Training, reading this book!
Negative staff attitude	Explain the vision, invite them to contribute
Existing CRM shaky	Training, reading or consultancy
Current reliance on very old technology	Outsource to technology consultancy and services bundled with e-Commerce services
Insufficient CRM staff	Recruit, train or start small with just top 10 per cent of customers and phase in

So what's the plan?

☐ Build intranet and extranet into the e-Commerce project

☐ Adopt a simple CRM system as a part of your business development programme

☐ Anticipate the problems and resistance to CRM

☐ Every customer-facing employee gets a PC

☐ Every customer-facing employee gets training on CRM

☐ Figure on getting CRM live within twelve weeks of the launch of your e-Commerce site (but only if you plan it in at the start)

Keep the intranet task focused

All kinds of systems can easily connect to your intranet and extranet. Sales, account management, customer service, production or operations management and even finance. But to get it working well it's best to work in phases – start small and grow as you go.

What should a good intranet do?

The system should help staff do the important, high-value parts of their existing jobs better, such as processing orders, automating customer communications or developing new ideas from customer feedback. Later, as the system develops, it should help them do new things that raise productivity or competitive advantage, such as automating production processes or project management.

A good intranet should focus on processes, not teams; on tasks, not documents; and on high- and not low-value activity (putting the internal phone directory on the intranet as the launch service has to be the most common cause of antipathy towards intranets).

Design the intranet as properly as the public site

If the visual design of your intranet looks worse than your public site, you're saying to staff, 'You matter less than customers.' While you may feel this is true, will they? The negative effect may be substantial. Besides, if you've already paid for a beautiful design for the public site, why not adapt it for staff? The cost should be minimal.

But when it comes to the layout and structuring of complex information on the screen – as it inevitably will – don't cut corners here either. If you're looking for productivity from your staff, don't expect miracles if they're clicking backwards and forwards, scrolling up and down just to find two reference numbers that used to live side by side on the paper order sheet. Invest time and energy in designing frugal, clear, swift processes for staff.

As a final design check, make sure you've structured the intranet around tasks, not the company structure. There should be no areas for 'sales' or 'management', just buttons saying 'orders', 'delivery' or 'complaints'.

Get away from documents and into tasks

A document is an end result. Even if it's a first draft, it's an end result. If your intranet is to drive up teamworking and efficiency, you'll need to get people doing a lot more than document sharing.

You'll probably benefit from getting the intranet to *remove* unnecessary documents. Imagine a sales order form – one copy to sales, one to accounts, one to production. Now replace it with a single 'add order to queue' function, which sales, accounts and production can view when the need arises.

Teamworking

Intranets easily cross departmental divides and encourage people in different teams, in different rooms, in different offices, in different countries to collaborate. And, of course, teamworking doesn't stop with staff. Teams that have customers on board (such as engineering projects, or legal deal making) can bring individuals together in ways that focus on tasks and outcomes.

Managing the change

It's your job as a manager to see that the cultural effects of teamworking are managed successfully. Unless you're communicating your enthusiasm for and commitment to this better way of working, the intranet will seem like a nice toy for three months, and then it'll slip out of sight and out of mind. You need to market the intranet to staff.

Host your own discussion area

When you host your own discussion forums, you're creating an area on your site for the sole benefit of your customer community. That's not to say you can't derive benefit from it – or even contribute to it. But the key goal here is to allow customers to express their views on your products and services, on you and on any other matters that they wish to raise (anything goes). Naturally, you're going to get a lot of complaints. Don't squash them. Act on them and then *show* that you've acted on them. This is an incredibly powerful customer-relationship management tool.

Here are some of the components of a discussion group for your own site:

- [ ] **A menu system:** This should allow customers quick access and search facilities into discussion on specific topics – for example: 'feedback on product A', 'new ideas for product B', 'latest fixes for product C'.

- [ ] **A simple interface:** You need an interface that customers can intuitively use, which lists queries and relates the corresponding answers in a familiar way (for instance, like the folder tree in Windows Explorer).

- [ ] **Real-time submission of messages:** Customers will not want to wait half a day while you approve or post their message. Incidentally, real-time submission demonstrates to customers that the messages are not doctored in any way.

- [ ] **An archiving system:** This should hold messages that are, say, over two months old. And it too should be as easy to search and operate as the main discussion area. Customers would normally be prevented from contributing further comments or messages to the archive.

But the nice thing about a discussion group that you host is the choosing of topics that you can set up at the start or add in as you go along. These may include announcements of special events, promotions, enhancements to products or services following customer feedback, publication of success stories (expressed in very factual terms of course) and other positive message making. A word of caution though – keep the content of what you publish as neutral as possible. If you start to coat all your messages with a sickly sweet taste, your customers will soon get the wrong impression and rebel or retreat from the group. Tread carefully!

Should you worry about libel? Obscenity? Censorship? In my view, no. If you don't trust your customers to be decent, create a separate area for the indecent ones. You can call it 'anything goes' so visitors are clear what to expect. Freedom of speech, even in a commercial environment, is upheld strongly by the online community, and they don't like it when new arrivals on their scene want to change the established rules.

One way you can decrease the likelihood of misdemeanours is by publishing a discussion-forum charter that sets out the rules of engagement. A charter isn't legally binding, so you can't sue anyone for breech, but you can at least make it clear what's welcome and what's not!

A few myths exploded

The gurus at www.intrack.com have some wonderful observations on intranets and extranets. Do take a look at their site. Their myths are generally aimed at IT managers, rather than entrepreneurs, but the meaning still holds true. Here's a modified summary of parts of their site:

1. Intranets are cheap

They are to start with. The initial costs in setting up an intranet may seem low. You find a spare PC lying around, add some memory and disk space, install web server software, a network card and you're on your way. This may be a bit misleading. If you expect your intranet to grow, be prepared for the costs involved with the growth. Before you know it you will need one or more of the following:

a) A faster intranet server or better web-server software
b) Increased disk space and bigger memory
c) Better programs, such as database interfaces, interactive group software, multimedia and other whizzy things
d) Increased network bandwidth
e) Support staff for managing your intranet

2. Build first, ask questions later

A lot of intranet projects don't take off as expected. Sometimes for a simple reason. People don't know or don't remember. You will have to use a lot of promotional techniques not only to get people to visit your intranet, but for them to keep coming back.

a) Request the help of your marketing department and use their expertise.
b) Promote your intranet through management. Have them mention it at all meetings and with all correspondence.
c) Hold an 'intranet day'. Give away prizes. Make a huge banner with your URL on it.
d) Update your content regularly with useful information. Add local news, weather, press release, etc.

3. Intranets are for big organisations

Not really. Even if your company has a handful of employees, you could use an intranet to your advantage. The success of an intranet depends on the cost savings and any increase in productivity.

4. Just another buzzword

Nope. Believe it or not. Intranets are here to stay. We will see different variations of intranet technology over time and we will also see this technology evolve, but it's definitely a permanent feature.

5. Platform-independent

Granted, intranets will work across a number of platforms. Your pages can be viewed by browsers on UNIX boxes, Macs, Windows and a number of other platforms. But once you get into advanced programmes and start using the latest technologies (Java, ActiveX, etc.) you will realise that you have to fine-tune your programs to support certain types of browsers.

6. Intranets require an Internet connection

No again. Your intranet can be up and running by itself without any connection to the outside world. You will still be using technologies that drive the Internet, such as web servers, browsers, chat scripts, news and mail servers. But you do not have to be connected to the Internet unless you want your intranet users to access content from the Internet.

7. Intranets require little maintenance

If you believe this, you are in for a lot of surprises. Intranets can grow really fast. If you don't have a good plan-and-growth strategy in place, be prepared to spend a lot of time on small, routine maintenance tasks. Adding new publishers, adding users, maintaining the user database, keeping the content and technology current, coping with growing demand for bandwidth, applications and information. These are just a few issues you will have to deal with. You'll also need a good set of policies in place. Be prepared!

8. Intranets are not secure

If your intranet is not connected to the Internet (*see* Myth 6) and you do not provide dial-in access, you have a lot less to worry about. Even with an incoming connection, you have a number of options to secure your intranet. Firewalls, SSL, password authentication, IP blocking and other techniques are available to secure your intranet from intruders.

9. Intranets are an IT 'thing'

Leave the control of your intranet in the hands of the chosen few from the IT team and you may be restricting its growth. Don't make it free-for-all publishing either. Let techies set up the system, but let management or marketing or operational staff manage the content publishers. You can also allow the publishers to use their own judgement and creativity to come up with content.

10. Intranets are internal webs

An intranet is not limited to a website. The technology is adapted from the Internet and the Internet is a lot more than websites. You can use simple technology such as enterprise-wide email, push technology, newsgroups, chat, etc., which are all based on web technologies, within your intranet. Why limit yourself to websites only?

Create a powerful revenue model

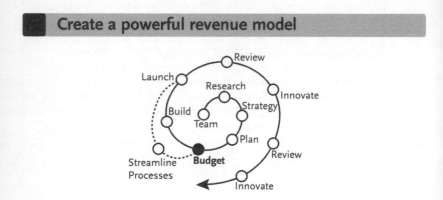

Every entrepreneur wants to know how much their website will cost. What's appropriate. The answer lies in how much you want to achieve. Know your targets, and you can work out your resources.

For me, revenue modelling is the basis of good e-Commerce. Your business is on a computer. Your customers use computers to trade. Precision is everywhere in your commerce. So the natural place for modelling revenue is on a computer.

What is revenue modelling? It's a spreadsheet that predicts the next, say, three years, with as many real-life factors as possible. Customer loss, seasonality, competitor behaviour, market segments, price wars and so on. It's not the real world, but it certainly helps you get a feel for the journey to success and the bumps along the way.

It's really the subject of a book on its own, but here are a few broad guidelines for revenue modelling:

☐ Set up a multi-sheet spreadsheet, and prepare to link lots of data together – the tighter the relationships, the more accurate the model.

☐ Create a 'product features and prices' sheet, which precisely lists every feature of every product or service you offer. If you're selling services to affiliates such as white-labelling, commissions, royalties or revenue sharing, then list these as services and price them.

☐ Create a 'market segments' sheet that puts numbers of customers into the various segments. Include here market segments you intend to reach over the next three years. This is the only sheet that is likely to have no dependencies on other sheets.

☐ Create a 'customer wins' sheet that predicts the starting position, growth and loss of customers in each market segment for 36 months. A useful check here is the market share you have at the end of Year 3. Is it higher than 1 per cent? If so, are you really confident that you have the marketing muscle to achieve this?

☐ Create a 'revenues sheet', which is simply prices times customer forecasting. Again, spread this over 36 months.

☐ Create a 'costs' sheet that sets out the direct and overhead costs for the next 36 months. The key here – and part of the great strength of this kind of model – is to relate costs to revenues by formulae. For example, how many marketing execs do you need per 1,000 customers? What sort of efficiency improvement will they make over the months (for instance, will you need five execs for 5,000 customers, or just two, because of economies of scale and increased skill?).

☐ Create all 'P&L', 'Cash flow' and 'Balance' sheets, and use them in your business plan

☐ Create an 'investment' sheet, which simply compares investment to returns. You can measure returns in terms of initial investment compared with dividends and capital gain at sale of the business (appropriate to start-ups) or you can measure in terms of set-up and maintenance budget compared with new business revenues (appropriate to existing businesses).

☐ Create a 'real world' sheet. In this, you load all your more unpredictable factors, such as price wars, competitors going out of business or attacking your customer base, underperforming (or overperforming) products, hostile community opinion, poor marketing results, departure of key customer-facing staff, seasonality, random effects and so on. Now you have a tool for creating worst-case scenarios and real-world effects. This is the sheet that you should really muck about with – see what happens to profit when the real world lurches!

☐ Finally, create an overview page to help you keep a bird's-eye view on the entire model.

So that's revenue modelling in a nutshell. Ask your e-Commerce consultant to help you with this if you're uncertain about doing it yourself.

Setting the right budget

How long is a piece of string? It's 10 centimetres, 1 metre or 10 metres! It's your string, so you choose. When you're setting a budget for e-Commerce, the budget shouldn't materialise from a study of resources. Nor should it be delivered to you in a proposal document by your web development company. You control the budget, and you should control it on the basis of your forecast returns. Naturally, that means you ought to have some idea of what your forecast returns are (if not, just read the previous section in this chapter).

Before we dive into budgeting, I thought we might take a quick look – as much for entertainment as for education – at how not to budget.

Budgeting Mistake 1

'We've got only five thousand pounds to spend.' This is cost thinking at its worst. No idea of the returns, or even why you're doing it. As the comedian Billy Connolly once said, 'You can buy a lot of Smarties with five thousand pounds.' What will you spend your £5,000 on? Graphics? Database? Content? How will you best allocate your money? How will you know if £5,000 is enough? How will you know if it's too much? If you're really strapped for cash, scribble down an approximate number on the back of an envelope, and keep it there as a check until you've actually set out your cash flow and revenue forecasts.

Budgeting Mistake 2

'Whatever the most expensive web company quotes – we will halve it.' This is market thinking at its worst. What if the most expensive web company is too cheap? What if they all quote roughly the same amount? Again, the back-of-the-envelope technique will probably stand you in good stead – map out your cash-flow and revenue forecasts and work back from there.

Budgeting Mistake 3

'Let's throw a lot of money at this – our future depends on it.' Diving in at the deep end has a big appeal to most profitable companies. Especially if management has suddenly become fired up about the Internet. Doing it properly doesn't necessarily mean doing it expensively. It may be that a minimal budget is all that is required. Again, decent cash-flow and revenue forecasts will help here.

Budgeting Mistake 4

'If we invest fifteen thousand in January, the site should wash its face by July.' Splashing out a huge lump sum at the start of the project, effectively denying the site valuable innovation funding or even simple maintenance costs across the year, is foolhardy. You should consider putting aside around 15 to 40 per cent of the development cost for ongoing innovations.

Budgeting Mistake 5

'We'll spend whatever our biggest competitor spent.' Dangerous stuff, this. What sort of resources does your competitor have? What percentage of business is online for them? What business plan are they pursuing – what aims have they? Unless you know for sure that you are comparing apples with apples, you may wind up grossly under- or overspending.

Budgeting Mistake 6

'We'll spend what we spent last year on the brochure.' Unless your brochure specifically delivered a measurable amount of sales or work last year, and you roughly intend the website to work the same way this year, forget it. Again, we're not really comparing apples with apples here. An e-Commerce website is a brochure, catalogue, sales desk, shop, meeting place, customer feedback mechanism, and dynamic promotional programme all rolled into one. Was your brochure really that good?

How to set a budget for e-Commerce

I hope the mistakes don't sound familiar! The simple message is, don't think about costs, think about profits! Forecast your revenues first, and then you'll have some idea of what it should cost. This applies as much to any part of business as to e-Commerce.

Now let's return to our piece of string. Its length is going to depend on a number of factors, business model, sales forecast and risk being the main ones. To a lesser extent, other factors come into play: how you want the site to support field sales, telesales or other offline promotional effort and whether you need to be compared with competitors' sites. Here are the prerequisites you'll need to be in place before setting a budget (they appear here in sequence):

☐ Choose the right business model
☐ Develop an effective price–customer model using a spreadsheet to set prices (see the previous section on revenue forecasting)

- ☐ Forecast your revenues, based on modest customer-winning and customer-retention forecasts
- ☐ Calculate your risks by creating scenarios where costs and revenues vary by up to 100 per cent
- ☐ As a rough guide, try to aim for the following results to investment ratio over the first year of operation:
  - ■ office model   3:1
  - ■ shop model   5:1
  - ■ membership model   3:1
  - ■ market portal model   5:1
  - ■ hybrid based on shop   5:1
  - ■ hybrid based on market portal   5:1

Please note: these figures are intended as rough guides only. Every business is different, and every website is different. I've based these figures on my experience and that of my clients.

Now let's look at some real budgets. The company names and their industries on the next few pages have been changed – but the budgets are real (and based on 2000 prices). I've added in here a time budget as well – because your costs are not just financial.

Company:	Hughes Jedd Ltd
Activity:	Agricultural machinery parts supplier
Site:	Online catalogue, B2B
Model:	Shop model
Profit Goal:	£100,000 within 6 months
Services bought:	Consultancy, e-Business Advice, Web build

Item	Cost	Your Input
Commercial Planning		
Revenue Model Consultancy	£3,500	4 days
Brief Business Plan Consultancy	£1,500	3 days
Investor Preparation Consultancy	£1,500	5 days
Total	**£6,500**	
Architecture		
Structure & Page Maps Workshops & Design	£3,500	3 days
Functionality List Workshops & Design	£2,000	1 day
Total	**£5,500**	
Production		
Visual Design Fees	£4,500	2 days
Software Coding Fees	£27,500	Nil
Total	**£32,000**	
Implementation		
Hosting & Domain	£500	Nil
Software Licences	£350	Nil
Total	**£850**	
Grand Total	**£44,850**	
Maintenance		
Technical Support	£450 pm	Nil
Content Support	£750 pm	Half day pm
Total	**£1,200 pm**	

Company:	Hayes Catering Ltd
Activity:	Premium catering for large events
Site:	Online order book and brochure, B2C & B2B
Model:	Shop
Profit goal:	£130,000 in 12 months
Services bought:	Consultancy, e-Business Advice, Web build

Item	Cost	Your Input
Commercial Planning		
Revenue Model Consultancy	£2,500	3 days
Brief Business Plan Consultancy	£500	1 day
Total	**£3,000**	
Architecture		
Structure & Page Maps Workshops & Design	£2,500	2 days
Functionality List Workshops & Design	£1,000	1 day
Total	**£3,500**	
Production		
Visual Design Fees	£3,500	2 days
Software Coding Fees	£15,000	Nil
Total	**£18,500**	
Implementation		
Hosting & Domain	£350	Nil
Software Licences	£150	Nil
Total	**£850**	
Grand Total	**£25,850**	
Maintenance		
Technical Support	£450 pm	Nil
Content Support	Nil	Half day pm
Total	**£450 pm**	

Company:	Hughes Jedd Ltd	
Activity:	Internet startup – car sales portal	
Site:	Trading centre	
Model:	Market portal	
Profit goal:	£1,500,000 in 12 months	
Services bought:	Consultancy, e-Business Advice, Web build	

Item	Cost	Your Input
Commercial Planning		
Revenue Model Consultancy	£4,000	6 days
Brief Business Plan Consultancy	£2,500	3 days
Investor Preparation Consultancy	£2,500	5 days
Total	**£9,000**	
Architecture		
Structure & Page Maps Workshops & Design	£8,000	7 days
Functionality List Workshops & Design	£5,500	5 days
Total	**£13,500**	
Production		
Visual Design Fees	£7,500	4 days
Software Coding Fees	£165,000	Nil
Total	**£172,500**	
Implementation		
Hosting & Domain	£1,500	Nil
Software Licences	£5,000	Nil
Total	**£6,500**	
Grand Total	**£201,500**	
Maintenance		
Technical Support	£1,200 pm	Nil
Content Support	£850 pm	Half day pm
Total	**£2,050 pm**	

How to apply for start-up funding

If you're looking to build a site or a business that's bigger than you can afford, you'll need funding from investors or a bank. Banks are likely to lend up to £20,000 for a start-up, and maybe £50,000 or more to an existing business. If you have good relations with your bank manager, then squeeze him for as much as you can get. You can always double your money with a Small Firms Loan Guarantee Scheme from the DTI. Have a look at their site for details (www.dti.gov.uk). I will ignore banks in this section, and just focus on investors.

Your investor is your first customer. You need to treat them specially. They will have wants and desires, fears and concerns, and you must address them all in a customer-focused way. Don't bulldoze: collaborate. Although you'll have to lure them with a strong proposition, you need to ask them what they want, what they like, what scares them.

Investors are interested in businesses that grow fast and, if they think your business will do that, put a decent price tag on it. If you value your company or project too modestly, you're losing money in the short term and the long term. You're bound to have a commercial negotiation, but, if your investor wants 20 per cent of the equity for 10 per cent of the company value, then you're selling out.

Of course, you can go too far the other way, in which case the investor not only can't afford you but also reads you as a bad manager if you can't evaluate a business properly.

I've worked with quite a few Internet start-ups and helped them to get their funding – and I've watched these entrepreneurs going through a soul-destroying process! Expect to give up some of your idea, some of your hopes in the name of a marketable success. Your convictions may feel 100 per cent practical to you, but, under the rigorous (and possibly ill-informed) eye of an investor, they may come out more like 50 per cent workable. However, don't give up. Stay focused on the success, the outcomes, the goals, and you'll ride the storm!

I've set out below a very brief guide to getting investor finance. Whole books have been written on this subject, but in my experience, and at the time of writing (late 2000), there is a 'best' way to go about getting investment funding.

1: Revenue model

Create a meticulous revenue model, on a spreadsheet. Use a modifiable set of assumptions (because you may get through five to ten drafts of this model by the time you're through. How to create a revenue model is described earlier in this chapter.

2: Business plan

Draft a very lightweight business plan for your own purposes. Try to keep it mainly to numbers, targets, very succinct descriptions of markets, strategies, etc. Calendarise your promotional efforts. I nearly always write first-draft plans for my start-up clients in a spreadsheet, not a word-processing document, because it forces us to keep it concise, and because I can link it to the revenue model (so it automatically updates).

3: Investor pack

Go mad on this. Make it the best document you've ever written. Use powerful, punchy language. Plenty of diagrams and stats. The very latest market research you can get your hands on. Design it beautifully. Try to get a single page to carry a single message, so the reader is in no doubt that you're focused, you understand the major issues, and you're not dreaming your plan. Consider at least the following chapter headings:

1 Executive Summary
2 The Opportunity for the Business
3 The Market
4 Key Market Segments
5 Business Model
6 Objectives & Strategies
7 Products & Services
8 Branding & Positioning
9 Management and Web Team
10 The Website
11 Premises & Location
12 P&L Summary
13 The Opportunity for Investor Returns
14 Next Steps & Time Frame

If you don't feel you can write a top-notch investor pack, get a consultant or e-Commerce incubator to write it for you. Make sure they've done it before and done it well.

4: Choose an investment level

Next, you need to decide how much and what sort of investment you're looking for:

Option A
Under £500k – smaller investment funds to support the site's build and general start-up costs. These tend to be available from wealthy individuals or smaller companies who will put in between £10k and £500k.

Option B

Between £500k and £2m – no-man's-land: it's very hard to get this sum of money without a working site or established business.

Option C

Over £2m – venture capital for marketing and operating a business.

You should try to decide whether your requirement is (a) or (c). If it's (a), then what will be your financial requirement for marketing the business in the first year, and staffing or operational costs? Think about these now, because, if you ask investors for seedcorn finance, that's the first thing they'll question, and they'll be looking for competent levels of financing in your investor pack.

If it's (c), then I would strongly recommend splitting your investment into two blocks, because most venture capitalists won't pump £2 million into an idea any more. Those days have gone. The institutional investor is less gung-ho on Internet opportunities, and generally wants you to have cleared a few major hurdles to show your staying power and conviction. Having a site, having a seedcorn backer, having a business already set up, even if not yet trading, are all clear signs that you mean business.

5: Direct marketing campaign

Next you need to draw up a list of potential investors. Group these into different types:

- Wealthy people you know
- Wealthy people you could contact through your social or business network
- Wealthy people you could approach through e-Commerce organisations or incubators
- Published lists of seedcorn investors (try the Venture Capital Report, available in most bigger libraries or specialist business libraries)

Now you approach your seedcorn investor list. Send them an NDA (nondisclosure agreement) and a lightweight summary of the business. When they've returned the NDA, then you can send them the full investor pack. This protects your idea from exploitation by dubious investors. Make sure you keep in constant phone contact, and that you're available all the time for questions, queries and further information. Push for a presentation meeting.

6: The pitch

Next, you need to be dazzling. Rehearse the presentation – keep it to fifteen minutes. Make sure you explain how much you're asking for, why, and what the investor will get back. Be prepared to explain what the risks are. Look the part – get a business suit or a new-media look, but stay smart. Bring your e-Commerce agency or web team leader with you. Let them tackle the heavy technical issues. Turn up early. Speak slowly and clearly, communicating the major issues in a concise way. Smile. Be really enthusiastic. Answer questions directly. Have a business card (from a vending machine if necessary). Create a rapport.

As you can see, this is all about being professional. If you're the entrepreneur, you're the business manager. Investors will be looking for superb management, leadership and communication skills, not just knowledge of the market, competitors and product. If they don't have faith in you, then they won't invest.

7: Closure

Finally, when you've pitched to maybe five or ten investors, you'll land a serious one. Now you haggle. They'll suggest you've overpriced the business. You'll explain why you haven't but show willingness to negotiate. When you reach closure, get a lawyer to clinch the terms.

So what?

You've taken a big step towards differentiation. You've planned a major advance on your competitors by building an intranet for staff and an extranet for customers into your project. You've prepared for continual improvement in customer service. You've built your service around tasks, not departments, and you've encouraged customers to express their opinions in a discussion area.

You've also vigorously checked your revenues and prepared a detailed forecast of sales, including the effects of seasonality, competitor attack, customer loss and other real-world factors. You've developed a sensible budget based on your goals.

Chapter checklist

Do I have the following?

- [ ] An intranet plan
- [ ] An extranet plan
- [ ] A three-year revenue model
- [ ] A sensible budget, based on revenue forecasts

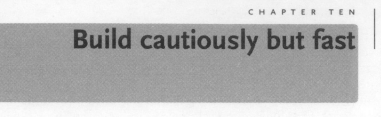

CHAPTER TEN

Build cautiously but fast

Building the site should be the icing on the cake. By now you should have good people, good research, and good strategies in the bag. Without them, you're about to throw away a lot of money.

Rush safely

The most common paradox for web businesses is how to get online fast, but safely. Most of my clients want to move quickly, but when they say 'within four months' and proffer a lightweight plan we usually suggest they halve the time scale, and double the caution. No one seems to appreciate how quickly the Internet changes, and how out of date your idea becomes before you can implement it. So we say rush safely.

How? By doing two groups of things well: speeding up and taking care.

Speeding up

☐ Generate a sense of urgency from the top – make it clear you're in a hurry

☐ Break down your aspirations into chunks, and split out into 'Phase 2' those that you cannot realistically achieve within twelve weeks

- ☐ Impose internal deadlines
- ☐ Release people temporarily from their daily duties
- ☐ Do not accept late work
- ☐ Get the web team to calculate their own project schedule which will hit your time scale
- ☐ Pass the urgency on to your suppliers and partners – set them deadlines too
- ☐ Move people on to temporary project attachment
- ☐ Work to a weekly calendar, capped at twelve weeks
- ☐ Attach more resources than you think you need
- ☐ Select your partners partially on a basis of being able to hit deadlines
- ☐ Monitor progress frequently
- ☐ Reward timely completion of good work
- ☐ Let everyone know they can take a one-week holiday after their contribution is finished
- ☐ Change the business plan and the marketing plan to coincide with your new time scale

Which industries are likely to need this kind of ridiculous speed? Probably yours! By the time you're reading this, the pace of technology change will be moving 3–5 per cent faster than it was when I wrote it. And I would forecast it to continue to speed up for the next eighteen months at least. Most entrepreneurs and managers think that, now e-Commerce has arrived, things will settle. Absolutely not. Watch out for live webcams, video customer service, talking websites, programmes such as Word and Excel running online, 3D interfaces and much more. Get used to the idea of accelerating change – before your more Internet-savvy competitor does.

Taking care

- ☐ Plan and communicate your plan – don't let the rush be an excuse for poor work
- ☐ Expect errors – and equally expect your team to fix them
- ☐ Meet frequently, but not for long discussions – keep the focus on sharing information
- ☐ Check your ideas early on with real customers and adjust them if they're not well received
- ☐ Check everything twice
- ☐ Hire the best-quality people you can afford – they'll help you avoid costly mistakes under tight time pressures

- ☐ Stay focused on specific goals – don't let the agenda wander
- ☐ Have a contingency plan for every major step of the project
- ☐ Test everything and keep rechecking customer or user feedback
- ☐ Do everything in parallel, not sequentially – this creates more time for fixing errors

So taking care is about being professional and thorough. And you're probably already some way down that path with your offline operations.

A guide to managing change

Most of us don't like change. It's unsettling. It's uncertain. And, for some, it signifies forthcoming redundancy. Luckily, most staff accept some of the changes required by e-Commerce, because they can see that the Internet is different from normal business. But, as a manager, *you* have the job of making people feel good about change, of motivating them during a difficult period, and of leading the change.

Good leaders have a number of important skills:

1 Good leaders set clear-cut new goals which people can understand
2 Good leaders listen carefully to their staff throughout the change process
3 Good leaders set high standards and expect people to live up to them
4 Good leaders encourage teamwork and good communication among all staff
5 Good leaders accept compromise only during difficult periods and then reassert high standards as soon as possible

Armed with these fine skills, you can lead any team through almost any programme of change. Let's see how they apply.

Change process

1. Explain your vision
Set out your idea of how the future looks. Describe it in terms that people can understand. Load it with benefits and positive messages. Here's an example:

'We are going to change our business. We want 25 per cent of our total sales to come from online customers within 12 months. We want all staff to develop warm, honest, friendly relationships with these customers through email and the phone. We want to feel less pressure, more fun in our work. We want to enjoy more profit, too. We want delivery times to drop to under two days average. We want to create an after-sales programme that keeps customers coming back for more and keeps them happy. We want customers to feel the change in our attitude towards serving them.'

2. Sell your vision
Once you've assembled your web team, ask them to improve your vision. Let them reword it. Let them add their own ideas and suggestions, but don't let them change the meaning. Now ask them to sell the new vision to their teams, to their staff. Let the whole company know that change is coming and that it's a good idea, an idea shared by all senior staff.

3. Agree a sequence of phases
Suggest a sequence of phases to your web team (you might like to use the virtuous spiral from this book: *see* Section Two: 'How To Do e-Commerce'). Let the team suggest dates, resources and budget.

4. Agree a schedule of review meetings
Set up a series of monthly meetings in which a wide number can contribute and learn of the positive progress that the project will make. The staff should act as your ambassadors by verbally relaying what they've heard at the meetings. This way, you can use the company grapevine to your advantage.

5. Congratulate the successes of the team
Publicly acknowledge the good work of the web team and other contributors to the project. Try to explain what the benefits of the good work are to the company. For example, 'Sam has suggested that we get the e-Commerce database to automatically email not just the order-taking team but also the operations team at the same time when a customer places an order. This should cut order processing time in half. Nice work, Sam!' It's obvious, but it gets the right message across.

Listen to the voices of protest

Listen to your production/ops team, especially if they squeal in agony! If they don't buy in to the new working methods, your site will fail. When you listen, try this approach:

- ☐ Listen without comment
- ☐ Paraphrase what you've just heard to prove you've understood
- ☐ Restate the objectives of the project
- ☐ Ask the protester how he might reconcile the opposing views
- ☐ Reach a consensus – try to adapt a bit of what they suggest
- ☐ Act

This is a reasonable approach to take with people who aren't ready for change. But sometimes you have to accept that your ideas may be wrong. In late 1999, I was doing some work for a food-manufacturing company, and the web manager was adamant that the big change should be Internet-enabled supplier management. Suppliers were to use a special site to bid for contracts to supply ingredients. The big idea was market forces on a micro scale. The operations manager put her foot down and no amount of negotiation would settle their dispute.

Eventually, we called in a few friendly suppliers to hear the two sides of the argument. The suppliers were most enthusiastic – they pointed out that the manufacturer's buy prices were already the lowest in the UK, and that a free market would really help them to recover to somewhere near average! The web manager slunk from the meeting and the operations manager was delighted to have been vindicated.

A guide to managing designers

Let's say you're not the most visually literate person. Your house is filled with prints from Ikea and you're renowned for wearing the loudest clothes in the office. Somehow, it's fallen on you to manage the web designer.

Two things may be worrying you. First, how will you get the most out of your designer? And, second, how will you know if the design is good?

Getting the most from your designer

The best designers that I've worked with have good communication skills. They listen carefully to your brief. They understand commercial issues. They react positively when your brief contains details of audience, message and competitive positioning. But many designers don't have these skills. It's your job to brief, motivate, steer and nurse your designer. Left to their own devices, designers have been known to produce beautiful work that is commercially useless. If you're in doubt about their work as it progresses, call in someone whose creative views you trust.

One of the quickest ways to get the design project running on the right rails is to follow these steps:

1. Prepare a written brief

It should include company or brand values. These should be emotional words, not commercial words – they should tell the designer how the audience should feel ('fun', 'listening' or 'shocking' are more useful to designers than 'value', 'service' or 'innovation').

2. Get two concepts

Ask the designer to prepare two concepts, so you have a choice. A concept is a first-draft interpretation of your brief, in the form of a homepage and a typical contents page. It should be rough, incomplete, but have the right feel. I always ask designers to provide their concept artwork at 760 by 420 pixels, so that I can drop them into a browser window to get the 'real feel' of a web page.

3. Check the concepts against the brief

Ask the designer to explain which concept is closer to the brief and why. This is an important check – if they can't, they've probably ignored your brief. At this point you really need to clarify with the designer whether or not you are happy with their approach. Ask a colleague with creative flair to participate in this meeting if you don't trust your own visual judgement.

4. Don't interfere with good ideas

Once you've approved the initial concept work, don't be disappointed if the finished artwork looks similar. Often, artwork that has a high impact is best left alone, the strength of the design undiluted by extra additions or secondary visual elements. Usually, the more tweaking, the less impact.

5. Keep your designer happy

Encourage and reward your designer – before the work is finished. Almost invariably, as their work draws to a close, you will find that you need a number of unforeseen favours, such as extra versions, variations for different departments, late additions of buttons, menu items, pictures or partner logos. You'll need to keep your designer engaged and sympathetic towards your commercial needs for these freebies.

Getting the best design

You can create the most competitive e-Commerce programme in the world and throw it all away on design. Whether you're designing in-house or hiring in design experts, you need to keep tight control on the visual design of your site. In no particular order, and with a little smattering of technical issues, here are the main dos and don'ts of web design. Break them at your peril!

1. Accommodate all visitors

It is impossible to please all people all the time. Every visitor to your site will have one of over a hundred possible viewing permutations on their web browser. Short of designing a hundred different websites, you don't have much choice but to make compromises on the visual and technical layout of the site.

Netscape and Microsoft supply around 95 per cent of the world market in browsers. Each browser comes with settings that allow the user to turn on or off JavaScript, cookies and pictures. Users can also set their own preferred fonts and colour schemes to override those on your site. Now throw in the possible permutations on 'plug-ins' (extra features that come as standard or can be downloaded and plugged in) – users may have animation, video, audio and other plug-ins. When you do the maths, you're looking at well over a hundred possible permutations!

So ask your designer to prove to you that the site is at least acceptable to the following:

- [ ] Visitors with slow-speed Internet connections – either minimise the graphics or create a text-only version of the site
- [ ] Visitors with small or poor-quality screens – even if these users are in the minority, it's worth double-checking that the colour and layout work adequately for them
- [ ] Visitors with old browsers – again, even if these users are in the minority, it's worth offering them an alternative site, which is perhaps free of JavaScript, cookies and Flash
- [ ] Visitors with Macs, Unix or other non-PC machines – this is a matter of running the checks on these machines; you may find the colours vary and strange things can happen to tables on non-PC machines

2. Keep it simple

Don't overload your pages with content, unless all your visitors are regulars, and you don't intend to win new customers! You must accommodate the first-time visitor, the low-tech visitor, the low-patience visitor and the no-time visitor. Clarify the site by reducing the number of options. Five or six main-menu buttons at the most, second-level navigation or buttons grouped to three or four, plenty of space round content and objects. These simplicities help the eye and so make it easier for visitors.

3. Work with a reduced colour set

Three colours well used is a better combination than a rainbow finish. Colour doesn't just appeal to the eye – it implies emotion, conveys positive messages like harmony and co-ordination. But most of all colour communicates logically. If every clickable element on your site is dark blue, the user will soon learn the significance of colour. You may choose for example:

Background:	Light or neutral colour
Text:	Black for clarity and printing
Links/clicks:	Dark colour, noticeably different from black
Emphasis:	Mid tone colour, for important content or headers
Separators:	Light tone colour, to separate page components

4. Keep payload to a minimum

Payload is the total combined file size of every component on a single page. Agree a maximum payload with your designer, and a normal payload size. Try to keep the maximum to under 40K (9.5 seconds' load time for a common 33.6Kbs modem!) and the normal to under 25K. Don't forget that the total payload is the combined file size of all the hits:

web page	10K
8 navigation buttons	6K
2 site artwork images	7K
1 product photo	8K
total payload	31K (over 7 seconds for a 33.2 modem)
total hits	10

Here's a table of load speeds – there are some pretty shocking stats in here. For instance, if your customer has a typical ISDN line, which is usually set by the installation engineer to 64Kbs, it will still take five seconds for your 40K page to download!

Item	Speed Rating	File Transfer speed
Modem	28.8 Kbs	3.6 k per second
Modem	33.6 Kbs	4.2 k per second
Modem	56.6 Kbs	7 k per second
ISDN line	64 Kbs	8 k per second
ISDN line	128 Kbs	16 k per second
ISDN line	256 Kbs	32 k per second
ISDN line	512 Kbs	64 k per second

5. Avoid frames

Frames are devices that allow parts of the screen to remain fixed, while others scroll. Even today, some search engines will not list framed sites properly. And database-driven sites are often more complex – and more expensive – to build with them. And, when affiliates or partner sites want to link to shortcuts or special doorways into your site (say to your special-offers page), managing them becomes trickier. So try to avoid them.

6. Squash pictures to a minimum

If you must use large pictures on your site, try to reduce the effects of unwanted delays. You can do this by warning visitors before they click of the file size they are about to download, and by compressing the images to the minimum acceptable quality. Nearly all modern graphics packages have facilities to automate this process.

7. Avoid dead links

Try to minimise the number of links you have on your site. The more links you have, the more opportunities there are for those links to expire. And the more checking and administration you're creating for yourself every month. Besides, when you think carefully about links, they are simply devices to transport your customers off your own site – is that what you really want?

8. Minimise scrolling

Unless you have a very good reason for it, avoid long pages. It's much harder for visitors to find what they're looking for on a page that scrolls maybe two or three screens. Visitors who have small screens – and that may be many more than you imagine – will thank you for cutting your site content into small, manageable chunks. To cut up site content, you'll need to think very carefully about navigation. The more cuts you make, the larger and more complex your navigation system will become.

9. Use shortcuts

Once your site has been live for a while, and you have collected statistics on which pages are most popular, it's a good idea to put shortcuts to them on to the homepage. Then visitors can make swift journeys to the most likely needed pages, without having to navigate. Shortcuts work well on content pages too.

10. Spread contact details liberally across the site

For the sake of convenience, and for the sake of trust, make your telephone number, email address and company address visible across the site. Remember, customers live in the real world, too! And, if you are trading online, you should inspire the confidence of your customers by appearing to be as open, trustworthy and contactable as possible.

11. Ensure that every page has a title

Search engines pick up page titles. So make sure that every page on your site has a unique page title. Try to be imaginative here. 'Riot of Colour Offers' is less clear than 'Riot of Colour Flower Store – special spring offers'.

12. Ensure that every page has a meta tag

Search engines also pick up meta tags. The most important tags are 'description' and 'keywords'. These tags pass information from each page on your site to the search engines. Again, try to use these imaginatively. For example, 'Riot of Colour – one of the biggest online stores for flower, gardening, garden furniture and horticulture enthusiasts' is better than 'the UK's leading centre for everything to do with the garden'. Why? Some search engines discourage the promotional use of the description tag ('the UK's leading' is more promotional than 'one of the biggest'). And you've cleverly managed to list four product types or keywords which people are likely to search on.

Frequently asked questions on design

Where do I find a good designer?

This is the wrong question. You should really be asking, 'Where do I find a good e-Commerce agency?' Design is important but it should follow the commercial logic and marketing aspects of your project. It should never lead. Besides, e-Commerce agencies will have a long list of visual designers and will always recommend an appropriate designer.

If you still seek a designer, then ask your ISP or local Business Link for a list – most of them have more than fifty designers.

Should we design in-house?

If you mean 'Should we do a DIY project?' then check Chapter 4 to see if you have all the necessary skills. If you don't have all the skills, then don't even *think* about DIY! Would you rewire your office without specialist help? e-Commerce is at least a hundred times more important!

Where can I cut corners?

If the agency you want is perfect in every way but price, you've got two options: cut the project or cut the quality. Most people try to cut the planning or visual design areas. In other words, they aim to build the same size of project, but with less money. You'll only get a poorer site this way. If the budget must come down, try to reduce the site size. That way, you'll keep the high quality, and leave room for development later.

Can I use my print designer for the website?

Unless they have an e-Commerce agency division, I wouldn't recommend it! Print designers are superb for high visual impact, but often flounder in the multimedia, commercial, strategic and functional aspects of e-Commerce. Use them wisely!

What should we put on our e-Commerce pages?

As a bare minimum, consider the following:

- ☐ Logo, consistent colour scheme and corporate visuals
- ☐ Description or slogan naming main service or product
- ☐ Navigation for main site
- ☐ Navigation for catalogue or service offerings
- ☐ A short description of the product, with a link to more detail
- ☐ A picture or illustration of the product or service
- ☐ Details of the options or add-ons for this product
- ☐ Price (and, where appropriate, conditions)
- ☐ Delivery and availability details
- ☐ 'Add to order', 'edit order', 'delete order', 'view order' buttons
- ☐ Contact details, including phone number
- ☐ Reassurances on security, credit card antifraud measures
- ☐ Money-back guarantee
- ☐ 'About us' section, describing the company and what makes it unique
- ☐ A description of products and services you offer customers

Should we use photos of our staff?

If you're in the personal-service business, yes. If you want to portray your directors or key staff as customer-focused and human, then consider it. If you have a strong 'team' message in your promotion, then consider a good team photo. Portraits are good for beefing up the 'guru-ness' or celebrity of key players. Action pictures are good for demonstrating how your staff work.

But, if none of that's important, pictures of dumpy staff in shirt-sleeves, with their foreheads glistening in your overheated late-seventies-looking office will surely convey a negative impression.

We should have a high-impact design, shouldn't we?

Be careful here! High-impact design is usually received by the audience as cheap, shouty and garish. Flashing icons, too many logos or images, large scrolling text, banner adverts, multiple animations, clashing bright colours and multiple large text all tend to convey an unprofessional, sell-'em-fast message. Let the designer advise you on what's appropriate to your commercial brief.

What is Flash?

It's a special kind of programming language that's based on animated line drawings. It has its own plug-in, which comes free and already installed with most modern browsers. Like browsers, every new release of Flash is better and more feature-rich than the previous version. And, as with browsers, new Flash files are not retrocompatible. So an animated presentation that looks great on the latest Flash plug-in won't run on previous versions. Be careful with Flash – not everyone sees it, or wants to. Some users switch it off. So it's a good idea to keep the Flash elements on your site to noncritical content such as welcome messages, illustration and brochure presentations, and stick to plain, boring static web pages for the critical content such as navigation, purchase and payment.

So much for design and designers. Ideally, you'll have them manage the constructors on your behalf. But if you can't for whatever reason, here are a few thoughts on managing constructors directly.

A guide to managing constructors

What happens in a typical project?

Here's a typical construction project, with its preceding architectural and commercial phases:

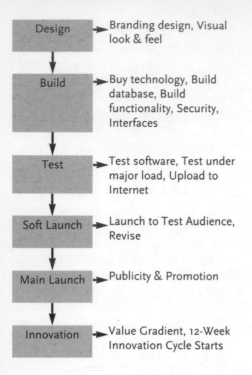

Design	→ Branding design, Visual look & feel
Build	→ Buy technology, Build database, Build functionality, Security, Interfaces
Test	→ Test software, Test under major load, Upload to Internet
Soft Launch	→ Launch to Test Audience, Revise
Main Launch	→ Publicity & Promotion
Innovation	→ Value Gradient, 12-Week Innovation Cycle Starts

To get your constructors alongside, you'll need to get them involved in the architectural stages, and also to use their time wisely.

They're a strange bunch, techies. Even the best constructors are not like most business people. On the one hand, they're generally propeller heads. Many have low or no social skills. They frequently can't explain their work, or present it. They think mathematically. They're individualists, not team players. They're reclusive, determined problem-solvers. They don't like people who change their minds and they don't like anything but the blunt truth.

On the other hand, they're highly intelligent, and understand implicitly your business processes. By the time they're halfway into the construction of your site, they'll probably know more about your order or production process and customer experience than you do. And you'll depend on them. So, if you're managing them directly, it helps to treat them carefully. More than any other group I've worked with, techies are so very responsive to good management and so blunted by bad management.

If you find yourself in charge of a group of them, or you intend to set up a web team, take care. Here are a few tips:

What turns techies on

- One-to-one recognition of their work, not just praise
- Your time when they need it, and listening to their ideas
- Not being dumped to the back of the queue on decisions or budget
- Clear briefing, including why something is required
- Patience and understanding
- Pizza delivered to their desks after hours (they're late-night people)
- Protection from corporate culture
- Diagrams of people processes

What turns techies off

- Office hours
- Team presentations
- Corporate regulations
- People in authority with no understanding of technology
- Low-tech when hi-tech would do
- Having to wear a suit
- Marketing people

Frequently asked questions on technology

If you're looking for a little more technical information, this section will dip your toe in for you.

What is a web host?

It's an organisation that hosts your website for you. They specialise in keeping the hardware and software working at peak efficiency around the clock. Typically, they will charge you anywhere between £100 and £1,000 per annum, which is a huge reduction in cost when compared with doing it yourself. Web hosts usually provide server space, security, and high-speed performance for your site. The kinds of conditions under which you might consider becoming your own host include highly customised database administration or very specialist security arrangements.

What is an ISP?

ISP stands for Internet service provider. Your ISP is the company that connects you to the Internet. They work in very similar ways to telecom companies, which connect you to the telephone network. You can't surf or browse without an ISP. Because price competition has slashed the ISP marketplace, most ISPs now earn their money from hosting.

Do I need a web server?

Almost certainly no. Unless you have very unusual technical requirements or very high technology skills and a 24-hour operation, it's much better to put your site on to a web host rather than your own web server.

How do I stop hackers?

There are two kinds of hacker. First, there's the just-for-the-hell-of-it type, whose reward is pride and entertainment. They're hacking in merely to see if it can be done. You're probably randomly selected or picked because of an oily press release about your company or its association with a hated major software company. They may leave a calling card behind – a virus or an unwelcome revision of your code that displays their name or message, just to prove to other hackers that they were there. Second, there's the criminal, who's looking for credit-card numbers or other valuable data.

How do you protect yourself from hackers? Use a secure server at your host. Nearly every host now has one. It's a special server which has encryption built into the way it communicates with the browser. So, as soon as a browser views a page on the secure server, it automatically switches to encrypted mode.

How do I stop serious criminals?

Serious criminal hackers will attack you if they perceive there's something really worth stealing. It takes a lot of time and effort to penetrate security systems, and if you have a major brand, with a high-profile advertising campaign, boasting thousands of credit-card customers, the criminal may develop a strong interest in breaching your security. So what measures should you take?

First, move your hosting in-house. This will increase your costs because you'll probably need 24-hour support and a reasonable-sized server. Second, put up a firewall and impose IP security (in other words, permit only known PCs to access your system).

How serious do I have to get about security?

This depends on what you have to protect. For most companies, a hosted secure server is adequate. It's cheap too – usually £200–£400 more than normal hosting. But if you have major assets to protect – perhaps thousands of credit-card customers and a major press campaign advertising your success to criminals – then perhaps you should consider a greater investment.

Can criminals steal money from my customers?

Yes, in theory, but it's nearly impossible. The theory is that if criminals can copy your customers' credit-card details, they can use them to make offline purchases for goods or to transfer money directly to their own merchant accounts. However, to date, I am not aware of any company in the UK whose customers have suffered this fate by online hacking. What normally happens is that staff intentionally or unintentionally pass credit-card details to another person or organisation using email. If their email is not encrypted, then hackers can more easily get hold of the number. Even then, this is rare. What's much, much more common is staff fraud. This is 99.9 per cent of the so-called online fraud that you occasionally read about in the press.

Can staff steal money from my customers?

Yes. I once had a client whose senior team leader used the credit-card details of her clients to buy a holiday for her family. She was caught, but, if she'd been careful, she might have been able to flee the country before the crime was uncovered. Your staff, of course, have full access to your customers' credit-card details. Whether they use online or offline methods, they have the opportunity to steal. This is the area you need to address the most.

What does encryption do?

It hides the message you're sending – or the web page you're viewing – in a coded garbled message. Encryption technology generally keeps several years ahead of code-cracking technology, so that all but the very wealthiest of criminals can't afford to crack your codes.

Of course, there is no such thing as perfect security. It doesn't exist in government, in the military or in your office! But, when you use good cheap encryption, it will take a criminal between three and six months to crack a single message, using top-of-the-range technology, working twenty-four hours a day, seven days a week. That makes it effectively not worth the hassle.

Where can I find help on security?

Try these sites:

- www.certco.com – CertCo is a leading online risk-assurance authority, providing the world's most secure e-business technology and systems
- www.verisign.com – a leading provider of Internet Trust Services
- www.128i.com – Public Certification Authority and associated support services

- www.entrust.com – security including training and consulting
- www.nai.com – security and tools
- www.pgpinternational.com – security company which also does encryption
- www.valicert.com – secure infrastructure technology for e-transactions
- www.xcert.com – Internet-based public key infrastructure

 ## So what?

You've understood the need for speed. You've controlled the most expensive part of the project admirably. You've managed change in your existing business, or introduced effective management to a start-up. You've sensitively managed designers and constructors.

Chapter checklist

Do I have the following?

- ☐ A change process
- ☐ A management process for designers
- ☐ A management process for constructors
- ☐ A live site

CHAPTER ELEVEN

Promote your site

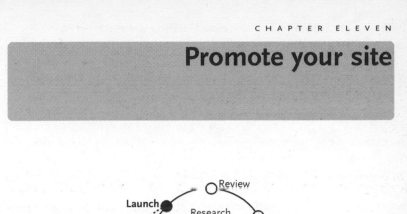

Launching the site is all about good promotion. There are so many ways to promote your site, most of which come down to message-making and good creative ideas. If you're not hot on this, don't worry – hire an expert.

What search engines are good for

Most businesses are dismayed to find that their attempts to be listed on search engines bear little fruit. At the time of writing, there were over 19 million website names. If you sit down and do the maths, even assuming 20,000 categories, that's over 900 websites per category! Small wonder, then, that you're not at the top of the list. On top of that, it can take over three months to get a listing on one of the search engines.

The consequence of this is that the typical e-customer will not find your site via a search engine. Let's look at this the other way round. You're daydreaming if you expect new business to flow in from search engines. That's worth repeating. Search engines are very unlikely to bring new business to you. So what are they good for?

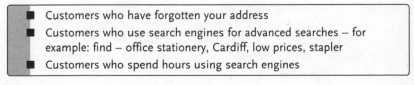

- Customers who have forgotten your address
- Customers who use search engines for advanced searches – for example: find – office stationery, Cardiff, low prices, stapler
- Customers who spend hours using search engines

OK, you're thinking, but there are ways to get to the top of the list – somehow to magically come up first, or at least to appear in the first ten. Most Internet magazines publish Top Ten Tips every few months on this subject. These stories make great reading but sadly it's impossible to jump the list. Just imagine if there were genuine tricks you could pull – then wouldn't everyone be able to? Then you'd be right back to square one again! Actually, I get asked this question so often by clients that I periodically email the search engines to ask what determines the listing order of their responses to search queries. They tend to favour sites that have been 'registered correctly according to our rules, and which most closely match the search criteria'. This tells you very little, other than to bother to register exactly as they describe.

How to get listed

All the search engines have different rules, and different methods of listing. And they continually tweak them. If you register your site and manage to get in the top ten on Monday morning for searches on 'orange juice cartons' on search engine A, you can be sure you won't be in the top fifty on search engine B. By Friday, you may not be in the top ten of either!

Besides following the instructions of every major search engine, to get your site registered correctly, you should use three key technical parts of your web pages carefully:

- ☐ Title – make this as descriptive as possible, e.g. 'Fulton Flowers – for Births, Marriages, Funerals and Special Occasions' is better than 'Fulton Flowers Home Page'. It communicates more to the user and much more to search engines, which will match on the descriptive words
- ☐ First text – search engines assign greater importance to words that appear higher up on the page, so try to get as many searchable words early on in the text
- ☐ Meta tags – use these to accurately and positively describe your products or services, without claiming to be 'the best' – some engines will blacklist you if you use the page description for advertising

Next, you should recognise that there are two kinds of search engine – spiders and directories. Spiders crawl around the web (hence the name), independently collecting information from every site in the world. There was a time when there were few enough sites for spiders to do this effectively. Now, because of the sheer volume, it's much better to register with a spider that will then visit your site independently. Here's a list of the main worldwide spiders:

- AltaVista.com
- Webcrawler.com
- Infoseek.com

Directories, on the other hand, are compiled by human beings. You must register your site with a directory, before one of their staff will pay a visit to your site to check whether it's working, and whether it's compatible with their acceptable list of business types. Most directories have categories and, when you submit your site, you must nominate your business as belonging to one or more of their categories. Some directories list only around one in three of the sites that are submitted to them! They may reject you for a variety of reasons, including abusing the description of your business by inserting a twenty-word advertising message, using any single keyword more than once, or leaving large parts of your site 'under construction'. Here's a list of the main worldwide directories:

- excite
- lycos
- yahoo.com
- hotbot.com

Finally, you could consider registering your site with the major UK search engines. These include:

- cybersearch.co.uk
- freepages.co.uk
- Internet-directory.co.uk
- isearch.co.uk
- ukindex.co.uk
- ukplus.co.uk
- searchuk.co.uk
- scoot.co.uk
- yahoo.co.uk
- yell.co.uk

If you're looking at these lists and thinking 'That's a lot of manual work', you're right! The worst part of it is, it's better if your company does the donkey work. There are shortcuts you can take; you can register with any number of registration specialist sites. But, in my experience, they seem to deliver less effectively than the laborious DIY approach. If you do insist on the less effective shortcut, try these sites for free or pay-for tools:

- www.submitit.com
- www.topdog2000.com
- http://websitesubmit.hypermart.net
- www.websubmit.com

Don't get blacklisted!

Some companies try to get their site listed higher up or more frequently by using 'cheats' – tricks to fool the search engine into thinking you should rank more highly. These include:

- Huge amounts of hidden words (say white text on a white background) at the bottom of the page – e.g. 'coffee bargains coffee bargains coffee bargains'
- Using numbers or '!' in front of your name to get higher up an alphabetical ranking – e.g. 01 Hexagon Hearths or !Hexagon Hearths, when your brand name is in fact just 'Hexagon Hearths'
- Changing your page titles frequently to get both the previous and the current page titles listed – e.g. Monday, 'Jimmy's Joists – Steel and Castings'; then, Tuesday, 'Jimmy's Joists – Castings and Steel'
- Repeating words in the meta tags – e.g. 'hot cars good cars fast cars cheap cars bargain cars'

Be warned! All of these methods will almost certainly result in your site being blacklisted. The search engines will remove your entry, and bar your domain name from being listed again – you'll have to buy a new one.

What online advertising's good for

Banner advertising is everywhere on the Internet. On the one hand, most of us regard it as an annoyance. Indeed, there are a growing number of websites dedicated to helping Internet users avoid the noise of Internet ads altogether. On the other hand, most businesses are attracted by the idea of low-cost advertising.

The kinds of companies and products that have successfully exploited banner advertising are as diverse as those that have failed. This can also be said about traditional billboard or newspaper advertising. So, is it something you should consider, in promoting your website? Before answering that, let's take a close look at what banner advertising actually is and how it works.

What is a banner ad?

It's a small picture file, which can be static or animated, that you publish, and it then appears on other companies' sites. When clicked on, the ad will take the user to your site.

Banner ads come in a range of standard sizes. Here's the Internet Advertising Bureau's standards:

- 468 × 60 pixels – full banner
- 392 × 72 – full banner with navigation bar
- 234 × 60 – half-banner
- 120 × 240 – vertical banner
- 120 × 90 – button 1
- 120 × 60 – button 2
- 125 × 125 – square button
- 88 × 31 – micro button

Typically, ads carry a company name, a product name, a special offer, special price, or other promotional device. They should always contain a 'click here' button to encourage the user to take action. The simpler the message, the more effective the ad usually is, and the more striking and visually different from the host site, the more likely it is to be noticed. But let us be clear on this point: you need your ad to conflict with, not harmonise with, your host site. This is a great paradox and one of the very best reasons why you should think twice before carrying advertising on your site!

How do they work?

When a user's eye is drawn up towards your ad, you have between one and two seconds to make your message work. If your ad is animated you may have twice that amount of time. If the user chooses to click on your ad, he has to depart from the host site when he is transported to yours. This is an important point. If he tolerates the switch from one site to another, you need to reward him with clarity and a more detailed version of the offer that appeared on the banner ad itself. If your ad merely transports him to your homepage, and he has to absorb a new menu system or page layout, you're punishing him by making him work harder than necessary.

For instance, let's say your ad promises 'Huge savings on bicycles! Click here'. The user should be transported to a single page which defines the special offer, perhaps illustrating three bicycles, each marked with 33 per cent off the normal price tag. So you will need at least one promotional web page for each kind of banner ad. Indeed you may wish to set up a mini website just to handle the banner ad.

What are the benefits and risks of banner ads?

The main benefits of banner ads are twofold: they help you to raise brand awareness, and they help you to increase promotional sales. Right away, it's obvious that if you have a small customer base and a low budget, or no desire to create promotions, banner ads are not for you.

However, building your brand or creating effective promotions may be an essential component of building your business. The first question is, how much will the business benefit from creating or building a brand, and how much will that cost? There is no straight answer to that question, but, as a rough guide, if your market share is lower than 1 per cent you may find it hard to generate returns on a brand-building programme – you're not likely to have the budget. And the second question is, what volume of extra sales could be created by an online – or offline – promotion? Perhaps it's easier to answer this question. You can always test a promotion on existing customers, or trial the promotion on prospective customers in a small, sample area or market segment. You might consider one of the following promotions for a limited period (say, a month):

- Price discount – say, 25 per cent off
- Volume discount – for large orders
- Restricted availability – available only to web customers
- Product B free with product A – encourages switching
- Free trial – a taster
- New product – launch promotion, be first to try it
- Lowest-price guarantee – match a proven competitor price

How much does banner advertising cost?

It varies. And, as click-through rates from banner advertising are continually falling, prices increasingly vary.

A rough guide is £20–£25 per 1,000 page impressions. This is for 'general' or untargeted advertising. You might pay more if you were advertising, say, text books to students on educational sites. The extra cost may be £10–£30 more per 1,000 page impressions.

Low-budget advertising

However, mutual free links and targeted collaboration are easy and effective. You could easily set up a 'swap' arrangement that allows you to place ads on your affiliate's site and vice versa. No money need change hands. Good commercial negotiation is going to be your best friend here.

In fact, this is the basis for many 'free' advertising services on the Internet, such as Link Exchange.

Where can I get help on Internet advertising?

Try these sites:

- www.linkexchange.com
- www.flycast.com
- www.247europe.com
- www.tsmsi.com
- www.realmedia.com
- www.nmms.co.uk

 **Use paper to promote your site**

First, let's take a quick look at the opportunities to print your web address on paper and other conventional items. You should consider at least the following:

- [ ] Stationery
- [ ] Promotional literature, catalogues, price lists
- [ ] Newsletters (online and offline)
- [ ] Advertising
- [ ] Press releases
- [ ] Signage/vehicles
- [ ] Business name itself
- [ ] Visitors' book
- [ ] Phone-answering machine and 'on-hold' message

Second, what sort of messages do we want to convey?

- Awareness (the web address is . . .)
- Benefits (what's in it for you, and where the web evidence is . . .)

■ Differentiation (why we're better than competitors, and where the web evidence is . . .)

■ Special offers (what's the offer, how long it lasts, and where the web details are . . .)

You may already have a promotional or communications programme running. You might like to review the messages you're pushing through this programme, and review them to incorporate these web messages.

But how many of these messages could be carried on the above list of paper items? Could the stationery and newsletters carry benefits? Could the vehicles carry temporary stick-on special offers? Could the signage carry differentiation? Could the phone answer machine carry special offers?

Using PR to promote your site

The purpose of PR (public relations) is to use the independent and trusted voice of a newspaper, programme or magazine to authenticate your message. For many businesses, it's the second best form of promotion after word of mouth.

There are broadly two main approaches to PR: hire an expert, or DIY. There are many books devoted to PR, and quite a few devoted to choosing, briefing and hiring experts. So I'm going to concentrate on DIY. There's a kind of sequence to PR, that's based on your own news-story frequency, and the publishing cycle of your target media. It goes something like this:

1 Go over your site with a fine-tooth comb, update it, refresh all the topical parts, revamp it if you need to. Make sure it's 100 per cent ready for the eagle eyes of the press.

2 Create a standard online press pack, which contains details of all the company's services or products, its management, its commercial performance, its location, staff phone and email contact details. It should also contain high-resolution photos or files that you might like to give the press to use in print (make sure they're CMYK not RGB format).

3 Introduce yourself to your target press on the phone. Try to establish a little rapport, and ask a few questions about the kinds of stories that they like the most, and hate the most. Be prepared for questions, even during your introductory call – journalists are supposed to be inquisitive!

4 Now you need a story. Something that is likely to help your target journalist sell their publication or demand audience attention. So

it has to be newsworthy. See the next subsection for idea on news-worthy items.

5 At all costs, avoid sending out 'non-news'. This includes announcements of records sales, new staff, a new website or new clients.

6 Next, you need to get your press release out to the right people. You can find an exhaustive list of media at www.mediauk.com. Draft up a list of the media that you think look appropriate, checking them for the audiences they published to, the kinds of stories they publish, their attitude towards the Internet and their features schedule – maybe they have a feature coming up in two months' time that's just up your street.

7 Time your press release to fit in with the publication schedule of your chosen media. Don't submit your copy too close to the dead-line because no journalist is going to bother with it.

8 When you finished your press release, add it to the online press pack.

What's newsworthy?

Here are a few general ideas on the kinds of stories that journalists regularly publish:

Create a benchmark
Publish a weekly or monthly statistic, which tracks over time the behaviour of your customers. For instance, an architect with a reputation for honesty and directness might publish a monthly 'tender tracker' statistic, which simply reports the average thickness of tender documents that landed on their desks during the previous month. The message here is twofold: first, clients, not architects, create red tape; and, second, we get a lot of tenders. It's light-hearted too, and most publications will warm to humour.

Publish a rant
Be controversial. Write an article that flies in the face of convention. Argue that black is white. Most journalists are happy to pass on your controversy and create drama on their pages or programmes by challenging conventional wisdom.

Hold an event
Arrange a conference – online or offline – based on a very topical theme. Invite the press. Make sure you have arranged controversial or expert speakers and follow up with a summary of the events proceedings. You get two major press releases from this – the first is the invitation or announcement; the second is the summary.

Present an award

Consider hooking up with a trade body or recognised independent organisation within your industry and either sponsoring or judging the entrants. You'll be positioning your business as an authority in the market.

Publish a report

Link up with your marketing department, and conduct a survey that is both useful to them and useful for PR purposes. Obviously, you'll want to hold back sensitive information or information that has commercial advantage, but why not kill two birds with one stone? If the analysis and the written report are provocative or topical enough, you're bound to get good coverage.

Online PR

Consider exploiting online PR. Besides paper publications and broadcasting, the Internet itself offers PR opportunities. Use a search engine to find appropriate ezines, newsletters and newsgroups for your particular market or industry. You might like to try www.listz.com, and www.deja.com, for a database of newsgroups and mailing lists. Be careful though – sending unsolicited messages is commercial suicide unless you've checked first that your material is appropriate.

You can also use the services of online PR experts, who use the Internet to target your press releases at their most up-to-date list of appropriate journalists. These are paying services, but are quite affordable. Have a good look at www.prnewswire.com, www.prweb.com and www.businesswire.com.

Using online newsletters

Email newsletters can be very effective for promoting new products and services, maintaining customer relationships, and building your reputation with existing customers.

Research shows (depending on whom you talk to) that between 10 and 20 per cent of all email newsletters generate click-throughs to a website. That's a staggeringly high response rate. Compare this with the click-through rate for banner ads of less than 1 per cent.

Probably the most perfect aspect of email newsletters is the fact that you're rewarding customers who have submitted their details to your site, with promotional material. Who says there's no such thing as a free lunch?

Let's have a close look at what's involved in setting up and running a newsletter.

First, set objectives

What is the main purpose of your newsletter? Is it to promote new products or services? Is it to enhance your reputation, perhaps by publicising your most recent successes? Is it a product in its own right, providing customers with high-value information that is not available anywhere else on your website? Is it a sales support tool that underpins your offline sales and marketing activity? Or is it a combination of these? Try to define exactly what the main goals are in producing this newsletter. Once you settle on one or two of these, then you can divide the newsletter into sections, each one addressing a single objective.

Second, choose a name

The name will appear in the subject line of the email that you send customers. So try to create a name that grabs their attention. If you run a gift centre called Golden Gifts, supplying corporate gifts to medium and large companies, you could call your newsletter *Golden Gifts News*. Not exactly eye-catching, is it? It sounds too much like promotional rubbish. The reader has to make a connection with the company name before she can register any sense of value in this email newsletter.

Perhaps a better name might be *Successful Corporate Gifts News*, or *This Season's Best Corporate Gifts* – Edition 1.

Third, create a schedule

Decide on whether you're producing this newsletter once a week, once a fortnight, or once a month. This will depend on your own editorial resources, and to a large extent on the audience. Try to establish what the audience expectations would be by asking them directly. There's no point in drowning your customers with news. If you're in the furniture business, supplying tables and chairs to interior designers, they may prefer a newsletter every two months, whereas, if you provide share information direct to the public, nothing less than weekly may do.

Fourth, define your content

Try to relate your content as closely as possible to your objectives. If the newsletter is essentially promotional, always make sure that you describe new products or services, their benefits, their prices, their features, or their forthcoming enhancements. If the newsletter is essentially a reputation builder, make sure you publish recent case studies, focusing on success stories and happy clients. If the newsletter is a product in its own right, make sure the content that you're publishing is original, provocative and what the audience expects. You may need to conduct research, or publish 'how to' guides, perhaps authored by the gurus in your business. And if the newsletter is to support your offline activity, such as field sales, telesales, or special offers, you may need to hand over editorial responsibility to those people.

Fifth, design your layout

Until you're sure that the vast majority of your customer base has high-speed access to the Internet, avoid using PDF, Word, or any other attachments to publish the newsletter. Use good old plain email. This immediately has the effect of reducing the design quality of your newsletter. Learn to live with it! You'll have to try the judicious use of capital letters, white space, and separator characters. Here is a good example of an email newsletter, produced by WebPromote, an excellent source of promotional ideas on the Internet:[1]

WebPromote Weekly April 2000: Volume 2
http://www.WebPromote.com

Feel free to forward WebPromote Weekly, the leading website marketing newsletter, to your interested associates.
To modify your subscription, please see Subscription Services below.

###

~~~~~ IN THIS ISSUE ~~~~~

* WHAT'S THE BUZZ: DEVELOPING MARKETING PLANS –
IMAGINATION VS. REALITY
* PRESS RELEASES ON THE INTERNET: NEW MEDIUM NEEDS A NEW
METHOD
* NEWS SPOTLIGHT: PANELLISTS MAP THE FUTURE OF ECOMMERCE
* NEXT WEEK'S PREVIEW

###

~~~~~ WHAT'S THE BUZZ? ~~~~~
http://www.WebPromote.com

* WHAT'S THE BUZZ: DEVELOPING MARKETING PLANS –
IMAGINATION VS. REALITY
Many Internet companies find it difficult to develop accurate expense and cash flow projections, with perilous consequences. Marketing's role in the process was the focus of a panel discussion at last week's Internet World, titled 'Marketing and Revenues: Turning Plans into Reality.'

---

[1] Example.

What emerged from the Internet marketing and finance veterans wasn't quite a blueprint to follow, but rather a wide range of pointers gleaned from the group's years of experience with numerous Internet companies.

The landscape has changed dramatically during many of the panellists' tenure. Lisa Crane says that when she helped develop Universal Studios' website, marketing asked for funding without being able to tell finance if or when the money would be earned back.

Crane, who's now CEO of the music website SoundBreak.com, says she's since learned a lot about what to expect when marketing a website. 'But back then it was all about experimentation. And I don't think that's completely over yet.'

Internet marketing still contains so many unknowns that Crane recommends marketers at big corporations 'keep everything under the radar'. At Universal, she says it was difficult to explain the nascent discipline of Internet marketing in terms that finance officers and other executives could understand. 'We gave them limited information, and lots of that was comparative information,' she says.

By Ross Brown
mail to: newsletter@WebPromote.com

###

~~~~~ NEXT WEEK ~~~~~

Cause-related marketing.

Check out the WebPromote website, with searchable archives:
http://www.WebPromote.com.

The WebPromote Team
http://www.WebPromote.com

Suggestions and article submissions welcomed at:
http://www.webpromote.com/suggest.asp

###

Let's say that you run a toxic-waste consultancy. Here's how you might approach your newsletter:

- **Objectives**: You have ruled out promoting your products and services, as they tend not to change much from one month to the next.

Instead, you decide to use the newsletter as a reputation builder, combined with a high-value product in its own right. The idea is to win as many new customers by word of mouth as possible, and in return for customers' registering their details on your site, you will provide them with a high-value monthly newsletter on toxic-waste management issues for industry.

- **Name**: *Environmental Productivity News* went down well with customers. Your own personal favourite, *Commercial Management of Toxic Waste*, was not as popular. You follow the advice of your customers.

- **Schedule**: monthly. Your customers indicated that fortnightly was too frequent. And bimonthly seems to you insufficiently frequent to build a reputation.

- **Content**: 30 per cent of the newsletter will be given over to case studies and success stories, based on companies who have recently implemented toxic-waste policies or programmes, and who have either saved money or increased sales. Fifty per cent of the newsletter will be allocated to simple overviews of changes in health, safety, storage, transport, pollution and other related legislation. The remaining 20 per cent will be relatively static information, describing in very plain terms the capabilities of the company, the experience of its leading consultants and the company's main contact details.

Selling into newsgroups and email lists

Let's get a few basics straight. Selling direct to newsgroups and email lists is very close to spamming. This kind of cold-sell approach is like bursting into the boardroom of a company you don't know, standing on the board table and screaming like a street trader. So be very, very subtle. We'll come to that in a moment. But first let's have a look at spam.

Spam

Spam is sending unsolicited emails to people who don't know you. You've probably received spam yourself, and, if you've received a lot, you'll know how annoying it is. Of course, there's a huge and powerful movement on the Internet, dedicated to stamping out spam. Many of the organisations that drive the Internet, such as ISPs, web hosts and Internet bodies, have drafted charters and declarations against spam. Yet many businesses still choose to break the unwritten rules of the Internet. Why would they risk doing that?

The Internet offers a global market with a single click. If you can send a promotional offer to over 1 million businesses for, say, £100, that's a pretty good promotional reach by any standard! And if just 100 of them respond (that's a strike rate of one-hundredth of one per cent) to your £50 offer, that's a £5,000 return on a £100 investment!

Suddenly spamming looks appealing. Of course, in return for your £5,000, you've conveyed a cheap, annoying, low-life, reputation to over 999,900 businesses. And you could have put your business at risk of being sued. If you have a reputation – or reputable products – you should avoid spamming at all costs. But should you avoid newsgroups and email lists too?

How to market to newsgroups

Sending unsolicited sales messages or offers to newsgroups (or public discussion forums, as they're also known) is simple, but tricky to get right. You're posting a message to a public group, and any member of that group can read your message. But, if the newsgroup is called 'biscuitlovers.alt' and you're in the biscuits game, it's pretty narrowly targeted. Here's a sensible approach:

1   Do your research properly and you may find a rich source of customers. You'll need to surf around a lot using your newsgroup software (Outlook Express, Eudora, Internet Explorer or Netscape Communicator). The software will allow you to make searches for specific newsgroups.

2   Ease yourself in. Don't blurt out your sales message the instant you join the group. Hang around for a few days. Get a feel for what's acceptable within the group. Try to build relationships with particular members of the group – after all, that's what a newsgroup is about. And, when you post your messages, always make sure that they carry your web address and your email address.

3   Repeat this process across a small number of groups. Don't join more groups than you can manage. If you have a big workload, try to limit yourself to around three or four. Remember, you'll need to keep revisiting the group every few days or so to be recognised as a group member. When you finally think the time is right to drop your sales message into the group, keep it brief and factual. And whatever you do, don't repost the message for at least another two weeks.

How to market to email lists

Compared with newsgroups, sending to email lists is more direct. You're sending an identical message to a fixed list of individuals. This, too, is simple, but tricky to get right. If the list is your list, and it's a collection of existing or prospective customers that have expressed an interest in you, then your email is likely to be met with interest. If it's a paid-for list, even from a highly reputable source, beware! Adverse reactions are very easy to provoke. Here's a practical approach:

1 Build your list. Take the addresses from registered customers on your site who have given you permission to contact them, or from offline sources such as phone calls and customer-enquiry or order forms.

2 Draft your copy. Decide whether you want to issue an ad hoc newsletter, a regular newsletter (say weekly or, more acceptably, monthly) or just a simple two-line message. Don't put important meaning into formatting – most recipients still receive only plain-text emails, and won't see your fancy graphics or animations.

3 Create an 'opt-in' or 'opt-out' device. This allows recipients to remove themselves from your list. This may sound like commercial suicide to conventional marketers, but, if you respect the privacy of your targets, you have happier recipients – and that's the idea here. 'Opt-in' is the best approach. It says effectively, 'We won't send you any more emails unless you opt in to this scheme.' Again, you're giving more power to the customer. An 'opt-out' approach allows your recipient to click a link or reply to you asking them to be removed from the list. On the surface of it, this appears to be friendly, too, except that two problems come into play. The first is that you've had to make the recipient work to get off the list, thus increasing their irritation. And the second is that those people who are familiar with junk email know that spammers love a reply – it shows that the email address is live. So how can the recipient know whether you're a spammer or just an ordinary company with an opt-out scheme? They can't – and that creates a sense of doubt or distrust in their mind.

4 Prepare a database of the email addresses and ready a dependable individual to handle any new subscriptions from the email shot (you have, of course, encouraged recipients to forward the email to a friend or colleague), plus the inevitable list of unsubscriptions from opt-outs or opt-ins. Note that managing an opt-in scheme is more admin work than an opt-out one.

5 If your list is big – say over 500 – you might want to consider using the services of online list managers. Here, you upload your list to the service, and the messages, and they do all the list cleaning and maintaining. Under no circumstances should you permit the list to be sold on – or sell it yourself. This is a breach of trust on your part, and it will undoubtedly backfire on you.

6 Now send your message, and wait for the results. If you've got a small list, you can easily use any reasonable email programme to send one message to groups of people using the BCC box (Blind Carbon Copy). And if you need to send customised 'mail-merged' messages, you can use a variety of mailing-list software such as Majordomo (www.greatcircle.com/majordomo) or Listserv (www.lsoft.com/listserv.stm).

Just to put the boot on the other foot, if you're the victim of spam, and you can't seem to get yourself removed from the dreaded list, as it's passed from one spammer to another, here are a few things you can do:

- Keep quiet. It's better not to reply to emails from organisations you don't know, since they will simply add your address to their 'live address' list and hit you again next week.
- Get busy. Use the spam filter settings on your email package.
- Get serious. Use one of the growing band of benevolent antispam services, most of which are free or very cheap – www.brightmail.com is a good one.
- Get angry. You could try legal routes – Virgin successfully and very publicly trounced a spammer in 1999.
- Get wise. Use any combination of these.

Where can I get help on lists and newsgroups?

Try these web addresses:

- http://listhost.net – Offers list-hosting solutions for newsletters, ezines and discussion lists
- www.oaknetpublishing.com – Advertising and list-hosting services
- www.sparklist.com – Delivers email list messages for businesses who wish to outsource their email newsletter (ezine) and email discussion-list hosting, management and promotion needs
- http://maps.vix.com/tsi/ar-test.html – Advice on how to test your system for vulnerability. The aim is to stop spammers abusing email
- www.greatcircle.com/majordomo – Majordomo – Programme that automates the management of Internet mailing lists
- www.cren.net/listproc – Unix Mailing Manager
- www.lsoft.com/listserv.stm – Management and control of email lists on either the Internet or private networks
- www.onelist.com – email groups (e-groups)

Optimise loyalty through reward schemes

For the time being, price is probably the single most important factor in influencing customer choice on the Internet. This is no accident, because, for many businesses, the principal motivation for moving online or for setting up a brand-new business online was to cut costs and thereby drive up profit and market share.

Prices of most products are lower on the Internet. A new breed of online shop has sprung up – the price-comparing 'shop-bot', which aggressively compares prices between competing suppliers, and encourages the customer to buy the cheapest. I have never seen – nor do I expect to see – a 'value-bot'. It seems that value has come to mean price. The one major exception to this seems to be in the provision of human services – this includes business services, professional services, and many retail services, such as plumbing, financial advice and photography services. In these sectors, most customers have a perception that cheaper is not necessarily better.

Today, many businesses that rushed to drive down prices are discovering that Internet price wars seem to be permanent. And as the range of Internet shops grows, making it ever easier for customers to compare prices, it's no surprise that the only winner is the customer and that the price of losing for suppliers is often business failure.

So what should you do? The most obvious solution is to differentiate – to add value to your product or service, by creating a wrapper of extras, which come as standard or as options. This makes it harder to compare you with competitors, puts you in a class of your own, raises your game. But what if you can't add value? What if your product is a commodity such as salt, T-shirts or light bulbs?

In the USA, many online shops now offer reward schemes. Most of these schemes offer points, unique discounts or cash in return for making purchases – or simply for being exposed to adverts. In Europe, at the time of writing, loyalty schemes are only just taking off. In the UK, the dominant reward schemes are 'Beenz', 'ePoints' and 'ipoints', and all three are in their very early stages of maturity.

It is forecast that two kinds of loyalty scheme will dominate: the first rewards customers by offering free or highly discounted goods from the same supplier. There's a kind of brutality about this – as a supplier is very obviously telling you, 'We want you to spend more money with us.' The second kind of scheme allows customers to redeem their points with other – noncompeting – suppliers. British Airways' famous 'Air Miles' is a good example of this kind of scheme.

The original idea behind Beenz was just that kind of scheme.

Launched in 1999, Beenz has quickly established itself as a form of e-currency – seemingly modelling itself closely on Air Miles. When you visit online shops and pay for products with your credit card, you will be rewarded with Beenz. Some stores reward you with Beenz merely for visiting (in other words for viewing their adverts).

ePoints is based on the same idea as Beenz, but its commercial background is a little different. ePoints are available only to NetBanx merchants, who have opened a store in the NetBanx shopping mall. Sounds restrictive? It is. That's the whole idea. In fact, the problem with Beenz is that any online store can offer Beenz – which means that your competitors can offer the same loyalty scheme as you. And what was the point of loyalty schemes again? Oh, yes – differentiation. The differentiation you generate by joining the NetBanx shopping mall is more visible – either you're an exclusive member, or you're not.

Finally, ipoints are modelled more closely on a pure, perhaps more old-fashioned, differentiating idea. To become an ipoints merchant, you must persuade ipoints that you're the only supplier in your category worth dealing with! Ipoints will then appoint you as the sole supplier in their programme for your particular business activity. The effect of this is to allow suppliers to clearly differentiate against competitors who are not inside the scheme. Naturally, ipoints tends to sign up the big brand names, such as Boots and Marks & Spencer. The nice thing about ipoints for customers is that they can redeem their points with any ipoints supplier, in a wide range of business activities.

It may well be that between my writing and your reading this, these loyalty schemes will have adapted and changed. ePoints already looks like widening its services and Beenz is already making strenuous efforts to become an e-currency. To get the latest picture, you should visit their websites:

- Beenz – www.beenz.com
- ePoints – www.epoints.co.uk
- ipoints – www.ipoints.co.uk

Love thine affiliate

Affiliate promotional partners

Finding the right affiliate partner can be a make-or-break decision. In a growing number of companies with whom I've worked recently, affiliates have provided a huge volume of traffic and new customers.

The beauty of affiliate marketing – or channel marketing, as it's sometimes known – is that your affiliate needs you as much as you need them. So a straightforward contra arrangement can usually be negotiated – you provide them with content, they provide you with customers.

Teaming up with affiliates takes time, but it's worth it. You need to find out what they want – in terms of both content and quality. You also need to find out what they can offer you, especially in terms of ideal customers and site traffic. The best affiliate shares the same broad customer profile as you. So choose wisely. If you've just set up a site dedicated to the supply of rare cheeses, supermarkets may, at first glance, appear to be ideal affiliates, but compare their audience profile with yours, and you may find a surprisingly poor match. Perhaps Oddbins or Majestic Wine Warehouse, with their huge audiences and connoisseur subscribers, would be a better match altogether.

Here's a checklist of ideal characteristics for a good affiliate:

- ☐ Close match of audience profile (e.g. same demographics, psychographics or personal interests)
- ☐ High volume of traffic on their site
- ☐ Desire on their side to republish your content
- ☐ Deep pockets!

Note that the best affiliate is not always in the same industry as you, nor need they be a very large organisation.

After you've identified a suitable affiliate, try to arrange a firm written contract along the following lines:

- ☐ The duration of the contract
- ☐ A clear statement of what they will provide you with in the way of promotions, editorial freedom and branding
- ☐ A clear statement of how their customers will be introduced to your website
- ☐ A clear statement of what content you will provide their site with
- ☐ A clear statement of royalties that you're prepared to pay for new business introduced from their site
- ☐ A clear statement of mutual advertising, editorial and publishing opportunities (if appropriate)

An imaginative financial-information site that I worked with recently set up two kinds of affiliate. The first was a pure promotional affiliate, such as newspapers, online information services and, quite unusually, competitors. They targeted their content at these affiliates with the intention of generating promotional benefits – winning new customers and generating publicity – through simple no-finance contracts.

The second kind of affiliate was a trading partner. Here, the goal was to secure a lucrative contract to provide high-value information to financial institutions who had perhaps fallen a little behind in their web development. My client – a publisher – could command good revenues from these institutions through a process known as a 'white labelling'. What happens is that the publisher licenses the functionality and content of his entire site to his affiliate. The affiliate instantly increases the quality and value of his own site without having to go through the development time and costs that the publisher has. In return he may pay a significant fee.

Offline sales integration

Locking up offline and online sales makes both activities work harder. Your website is not separate from your business, so your online promotion should not run independently of your offline.

Let's set aside paper, which we've already dealt with in an earlier part of this chapter. We'll concentrate just now on field sales, telesales and networking. But first, let's explore what online activities can tie up with these human activities.

Homepage public promotion

It almost goes without saying, but if you're running a special offer on the site it should be in two places – on the homepage and on the lips of your sales people (and all customer-facing staff).

Online evidence pack

This is the first of the 'private pages'. The idea here is that you gather together a range of specific case studies and success stories, to meet the needs of most possible sales situations. You would normally bundle a careful selection of these into a tailor-made A4 pack. Maybe you need twenty or thirty. You fix these addresses with the web management team, but don't publish them anywhere on your site, or on search engines. There's nothing particularly valuable about these pages, but they're hidden from the rest of the world. You could even remove the sales gloss from them, and give them the appearance of training materials for your staff, maybe even password-protect them.

Now, you pass on the addresses – usually one or two only – in a discreet manner to your prospective customer, who perceives they have 'inside information'. And they do.

Special offers

This can be another 'private page', or it can be public, with a link from the homepage. Here, you're setting up a promotional offer for all prospective customers. It can be a simple taster of your main product or service, or a large time-limited offer. The details, terms and conditions are all on the page, together with a small 'register now' form, which prospective customers must complete to participate.

Again, you pass on the details to your prospective customer, and invite them to register. It helps if you have a printed paper version of the offer for those who are too busy, or not sufficiently web-savvy to log on.

Targeted promotion

This is more likely to be effective if it's a 'private page'. You set up a special promotion targeted at a specific segment or group of customers. You need to synchronise this with a sales targeting programme.

Now, when you meet prospects, you can pass on the address. You could reinforce the promotion with a DTP'd version of the offer too.

Custom promotion for big targets

This approach is worth it if you're chasing a large customer. You might set up a special one-off area on the site just for them. It might contain a collection of relevant case studies, presentations, names and pictures of your staff, proposed terms and conditions – you can tailor almost any amount of information for this pitch.

You might hand over the address and password in advance of meeting them, or present the entire package on their premises. Or you might do both.

Family silver – proprietary systems and processes

Here you're demonstrating highly valuable secrets. These could be 'your way of working', bright ideas for forthcoming products, unique systems or processes that you've carefully developed over the years, or an in-depth explanation of what makes you different. Definitely something you want to protect!

Unlike with the evidence pack, you don't hand over the password details. You demo this live in your client's office. Even today, it still impresses customers when you make a presentation on their systems, without using anything you've brought to the meeting!

Extranet

Finally, you can demo a live system. The customer extranet. You can give them a feel of what it will be like for them when they sign on the dotted line. You can walk them through products and features and prove to them that it all works. You can even (with permission of course) dip into another customer's account to show how they've exploited the system to full advantage.

Now let's examine which elements of these activities can be locked to online activity:

	Online Evidence	Special Offers	Targeted Promotion	Custom Promotion	Family Silver	Extranet
Field sales people visit customers at their premises. They meet face to face, develop personal relationships, and make reassuring (sometimes over-enthusiastic!) promises. Their game is about matching a solution to a problem.	Y		Y	Y	Y	Y
Telesales people call customers at their premises. They establish verbal rapport for around 2–10 minutes per call. They usually work from a milestone-based sequence towards closure. Their game is usually about maximising results while minimising time.	Y	Y	Y	Y		
Networkers meet customers through mutual contacts, and rarely at the customers' premises. They deal in the currency of benevolence, of connecting 'givers' with 'getters'. Their game is all about establishing trust and rapport.	Y				Y	Y

Coping with sales decline

Many of us grow our businesses by determination. Some of us are lucky and the customers come banging at our doors. But we all hit a dry patch from time to time. In e-Commerce, this is more scary. We start to ask, 'Is it the site?', 'Is it a wave of dissent in our customer community?', 'Is it competitor attack?' The possible causes seem further beyond us, because we're exposed to the vagaries of a wider and vocal marketplace, one with teeth.

If you hit such a patch, I suggest you avoid self-doubt and jump straight into a few checks on offline sales. Have they nose-dived too? If so, it's quite possible your offline promotional work isn't delivering. So what should you do? Get off your knees and get on to the options!

I've set out a list of sales tips here (many borrowed from the excellent *Ultimate Entrepreneur's Book* by Richard Dobbins and Barrie Pettman – thank you). They appear in no particular order of importance, and without online/offline labels. Some are quick fixes, some are long-term. Not all will work for you, and not all will be appropriate for any given circumstance. Choose wisely. And remember: none of them work without energy!

Promotion

- ☐ Simplify your promotional message
- ☐ Convert features into benefits in your sales messages
- ☐ Ask your twenty best customers for a glowing testimonial
- ☐ Smarten up your image
- ☐ Smarten up your documents and presentations
- ☐ Smarten up your website
- ☐ Send out more brochures, letters and flyers
- ☐ Send more email newsletters or promotional offers
- ☐ Develop a focused PR programme (over six months)
- ☐ Try some highly targeted advertising (over six months)
- ☐ Send Christmas cards or birthday cards to your producers, not your customers

Special offers

- ☐ Free samples
- ☐ Thirty-day free trial
- ☐ Volume discounts
- ☐ Free offer if customer promises to spend £X in Y months
- ☐ Reduction off next purchase
- ☐ Money-back guarantee if not satisfied
- ☐ Free maintenance and service
- ☐ Extended guarantees
- ☐ Matching purchase – buy an X, why not get Y, which matches?

Price

- [ ] Increase price by 10 per cent (the market can often take it)
- [ ] Reduce your price by 5 per cent if you're leading the market
- [ ] Offer credit facilities
- [ ] Set up direct debit facilities

Positioning and reputation

- [ ] Redefine your positioning – be Number 1 in your own class
- [ ] Amplify the best attributes your customers think you have

Distribution/channel marketing

- [ ] Use a big distributor
- [ ] Franchise your business idea to other sales territories
- [ ] License your product to competitors or other companies
- [ ] Joint ventures with other businesses to sell your wares
- [ ] Locate close to a competitor – build on their business

Value

- [ ] Hike up functional benefits of your product/service by just 10 per cent
- [ ] Raise perceived benefits of your product/service by just 10 per cent
- [ ] Lower your price by 5 per cent compared with market average

Segmentation

- [ ] Sell to more of the same kinds of customer
- [ ] Sell more products to the same existing customers
- [ ] Sell different products to the same existing customers
- [ ] Sell the same products to new markets
- [ ] Focus more – stop serving the most unprofitable customers

Leads

- [ ] Follow up every lead
- [ ] Ask all but your worst 20 per cent of customers for a referral

- [ ] Ask a receiver for lists of customers of a collapsing business
- [ ] Contract with a receiver to take over those customers
- [ ] Ask your suppliers for leads
- [ ] Ask your affiliates for leads
- [ ] Ask your bank manager for leads
- [ ] Ask your accountant for leads
- [ ] Join newsgroups and build a list of potential prospects

Service

- [ ] Improve service levels
- [ ] Be more polite and respectful to customers
- [ ] Listen to customer complaints more closely, then fix the problems
- [ ] Create a customer account plan for your top 20 per cent of customers
- [ ] Be faster
- [ ] Be friendlier
- [ ] Be more stylish
- [ ] Make choosing, ordering and paying all easier
- [ ] Change the attitude of customer-facing staff

Competitors

- [ ] Adapt and improve on ideas that your competitors have
- [ ] Swap dead leads with a competitor
- [ ] Join forces with a competitor to see if bigger is more appealing
- [ ] Competitor research – ask customers to compare your product
- [ ] Competitor research – ask customers to compare your business

Sales process and closing

- [ ] Create a ten-step selling process (starting with lead generation and ending with sales closure)
- [ ] Get better at negotiation – turn objections into opportunities
- [ ] Get better at closing sales
- [ ] Get better at canvassing for new leads
- [ ] Get better at providing engaging sales-development activities
- [ ] Send every salesperson on a sales refresher course

- [ ] Recruit more salespeople
- [ ] Recruit better salespeople
- [ ] Recruit commission-only salespeople
- [ ] Monitor sales effectiveness and reward the best
- [ ] Pay higher sales commission
- [ ] Recontact old customers
- [ ] Recontact old sales leads
- [ ] Build a network of contacts and collaborate on sales
- [ ] Build a network of customers and encourage them to trade
- [ ] Up-sell higher quality and higher price to existing customers
- [ ] Cross-sell complementary products at point of purchase
- [ ] Post-sell – during follow-up phone calls after the first sale
- [ ] Sell to other people's customers who have a similar audience
- [ ] Telesales campaign
- [ ] Telesales call after a mailshot or email shot usually increases the strike rate

Product

- [ ] Buy someone else's phasing-out product and resurrect it

Events

- [ ] Organise a conference on a topical issue
- [ ] Organise a specialist training conference for, say, chemists or managers

So what?

You've put together your first draft of a major promotional programme. That's more than most online businesses. You've been thorough, positive and vigorous in your consideration of all the options for your site.

Chapter checklist

Do I have the following?

- [ ] My site registered with the search engines
- [ ] A decision on whether banner advertising is appropriate

- [ ] A paper-based promotional programme to attract traffic to the site
- [ ] Our web address on everything our customer sees
- [ ] An outline PR programme which we can do ourselves
- [ ] A list of suitable online PR targets
- [ ] A draft online newsletter
- [ ] An outline loyalty programme
- [ ] A list of potential affiliates
- [ ] A draft contract for affiliates
- [ ] An offline sales programme

CHAPTER TWELVE

Grow your business, grow your site

Review before you innovate! It seems obvious, but, with so much pressure to change, sometimes even the best businesses adjust their sites too frequently, and without checking customer feedback first.

Fire, aim, fire, aim, fire, aim. Conventional marketing has it the other way round. You plan – you take aim. You implement – you fire. Now the only problem with this is that the plan is not real – it's just a plan. In the real world, things go wrong. Things are unpredictable. And the only reason that convention has evolved this way is because it's expensive not to plan. Because we want to predict the outcomes of our efforts accurately. We want to win, and influence our chances of winning. So how do we win?

Well the question is wrong. The idea is flawed, at least in part. Winning is an event in sports or games. It happens at the end, after all competitors have done their best. But there is no winner in business. There's no winning event. Businesses – online or offline – don't actually win. They get ahead. They lead, at most. But the game is never over (unless of course you're bust!).

So 'winning' should really read 'leading'. Now let's re-ask the question. How do we lead?

> Start the race (get into the market first), write the rules, blaze the trail, attract all the customers and build huge barriers to entry; or
>
> join the race at any point, learn the rules, stay on course and accelerate until you reach the front of the field

Ninety-nine point nine per cent of companies do it the second way. This book is largely given over to the second way. But the most important part of this is staying on course. This is the true test of good management; keeping the programme on track while under pressure.

Track your progress

If you prepared before you started (as described in Chapter 6), you'll have targets like these:

- Online sales or orders worth £X by Y date
- Online live customers worth £X by Y date
- Online repeat customers worth £X by Y date
- Online new customers worth £X by Y date
- Online vocal customers worth £X by Y date
- Online referrals worth £X by Y date

Let's say it's three months into the twelve-month programme and your sales are worth a combined total of £Z – is that good news or bad? Of course, your annual targets don't help – you need calendarised forecasts. And they need to follow real-world events, which take account of seasonality, customer loss and other predictable events such as sales promotions or launches. Of course, no one can predict the unpredictable, and no sales forecast should contain specific random effects. However, it's helpful to estimate a few likely effects.

Let's say your online Year 1 target is £240k. That's £20k per month, isn't it? Definitely not! So, if we've achieved revenues of £60k by Month 3, are we doing OK? Let's look at the effect of real-world events on our tracking system:

Even spread of annual target		Effect of slow brand takeup		Seasonal effect		Effect of customer loss		Effect of sales promos		Adjusted Monthly Target	
		%	£k	%	£k	%	£k	%	£k	Mth	Cumul
Jan	20	−55%	−11	−20%	−4	0%	−	11%	2	7	7
Feb	20	−45%	−9	10%	2	−1%	−0	11%	2	15	22
Mar	20	−35%	−7	15%	3	−2%	−0		−	16	38
Apr	20	−25%	−5	15%	3	−3%	−	1	−	17	55
May	20	−15%	−3	10%	2	−4%	−1	11%	2	20	76
Jun	20	−5%	−1	10%	2	−5%	−1	11%	2	22	98
Jul	20	5%	1	−25%	−5	−6%	−1		−	15	113

Even spread of annual target		Effect of slow brand takeup		Seasonal effect		Effect of customer loss		Effect of sales promos		Adjusted Monthly Target	
		%	£k	%	£k	%	£k	%	£k	Mth	Cumul
Aug	20	15%	3	−25%	−5	−7%	−1		−	17	129
Sep	20	25%	5	10%	2	−8%	−2	11%	2	28	157
Oct	20	35%	7	20%	4	−9%	−2	11%	2	31	188
Nov	20	45%	9	15%	3	−10%	−2		−	30	218
Dec	20	55%	11	−35%	−7	−11%	−2		−	22	240

The per cent figures are your estimated or forecast effect on the 'even spread' monthly figure in Column 2. For example, you want to forecast the effect of slow brand awareness, building gradually over the year. In Month 1, when awareness is lowest, you might knock 55 per cent off the value of the even spread figure of £20k. That's £11k gone, just because people don't know who you are.

To answer our Month 3 question, £60k is a quarter of the year's revenue at a quarter of the year mark. But it's much better than the £38k real-world target. So we're doing very well!

Now that you have a decent forecaster for your targets, you can track progress pretty accurately. We use this system in our office, and it works very well.

Corrective action

But what happens when reality veers off the planned path? A competitor blows you out of the water, for instance. There's an economic downturn. You've hopelessly overestimated sales. Customers are scared off your product or service by protest groups. The press attacks you. Global players enter the market. European legislation cripples your costs. It could be anything. What do you do? Well, of course, you react. You get on the case and take corrective measures.

Here are the kinds of decisions you should take, in order of desperation:

- [ ] Set aside a 15 per cent contingency budget as a part of the overall project budget
- [ ] Try harder with existing resources – motivate your team to deliver better results (use personal encouragement, work longer hours, roll up your sleeves and get stuck in yourself), use the same equipment, computers and production processes more efficiently

- [ ] Get more resources – hire more staff or subcontractors, buy or hire more equipment and throw more into the overall effort, and carefully control costs (use the money from the contingency budget for this)
- [ ] Step over the contingency budget and make a plea to the financial controller for more funds
- [ ] Reduce the targets in the plan and revise the profit forecast; consider launching alternative products or services quickly; accept that you will take a hit
- [ ] Reassign important people or equipment to more profitable areas and consider large-scale reorganisation of the product or service portfolio
- [ ] Take emergency measures – shut down departments, lay off staff, sell parts of the company or other major assets

Of course, the place to make these decisions is in a management or senior meeting. And then, afterwards, you have to implement the decisions, in the most positive way possible. It's all part of being a manager, or an entrepreneur. The rough with the smooth, the risk with the reward.

Of course, the relief for web-based businesses is that change can be a lot quicker on the site than in the real world. Enterprises that sell software or information may well find it easier to change because everything's online and reconfigurable.

Greater evils

Here are a few of my favourite alarm bells. They ring whenever I encounter one or more of the following:

- [ ] Sites without targets
- [ ] Revenues without models
- [ ] Entrepreneurs without plans
- [ ] Business plans without marketing plans (should be about 60 per cent of it!)
- [ ] Directors without computers
- [ ] Prices without research
- [ ] e-Commerce without marketing budget
- [ ] Technology without people
- [ ] Users without stereotype segmentation
- [ ] Targets such as 10 per cent market share in Year 1
- [ ] Start-up sites hosted in-house

- [ ] Construction budget bigger than 10 times the planning/architecture budget
- [ ] Persistent 'e-Commerce is IT' attitude
- [ ] Business plan written by a finance expert

Lesser evils

And here are a few of the smaller alarm bells:

- [ ] No computer-literate staff
- [ ] A comprehensive specification document before revenue planning
- [ ] Sales team want the site to generate new leads
- [ ] No one's seen any competitor sites
- [ ] Multiple suppliers for e-Commerce, planning, strategy and design
- [ ] Microsoft products as a pre-project prerequisite

Build to last

Innovation is the final piece to the e-Commerce jigsaw. Innovation isn't a face-lift: it's an improvement of value. And that's where your focus should lie.

Many businesses apply traditional planning and development cycles to the web. Big mistake! You may be used to planning and developing your product on a fixed time scale. It's a familiar process. But with e-Commerce you're not building a normal product. It's not a one-off. You're building a living, growing, changing centre for trade.

Your customers should influence the site's content as much as you do. It will need additions, removals, overhauls, facelifts and major surgery.

And, if you do a good job, it will probably outlast every product you've ever sold. So it helps if you think of it as a Lego set rather than a model plane. It's reconfigurable, not fixed.

So how do you make it so flexible?

- [ ] Expect to make changes; don't regard anything as permanent
- [ ] Before the site is built, ask the designer and constructors to design in flexibility (e.g. easily change the homepage, catalogue, photo or text content, navigation system and even colour schemes)
- [ ] Ramp up small but continual improvements to your products and services
- [ ] Introduce brand-new products and services
- [ ] Continually and gently increase the functionality (buttons and actions) on your site
- [ ] Tie yourself to your communities and act on their suggestions for improvement
- [ ] Tie yourself to your affiliates and act on their suggestions for joint promotion, or response to market trends
- [ ] Encourage your offline sales people to influence your site

But building to last isn't just about continual development. Many of the rules of Internet marketing in Chapter 3 apply here. If you can put in play even half of these, you're well on your way to a lasting e-Commerce site:

1. Internet marketing is 90 per cent product, 10 per cent perception
Put content in front of design or presentation. Focus on pricing, distribution and delivery, then finally presentation.

2. Customers buy benefits and proofs
Every page on your site should explain how your product will solve your customer's problem, and demonstrate it using proof.

3. Internet business returns are long term
e-Commerce is a long-term game. Invest wisely and don't expect payback for around twelve months. It's better to work in smaller, well-planned phases, so you can inch up customer service and delivery in parallel with the site's development.

4. Internet marketing comes from the whole company, not just sales
Put convenience, speed, hospitality, choice, proactivity, manners and honesty into everyone's brief, not just the sales team's. Build the whole company around the customer and their approach to buying from you.

5. Be different – be your own Number 1
Be Number 1 in your own, self-defined category. Because, in a field of one, you're the top player!

6. The management team drives e-Commerce
Drive all your Internet efforts from the top. Think long-term, integrate everything online with everything offline. Plan. Take control.

7. Success and failure are both necessary
If you don't fail occasionally then you're not taking enough risks. When you do encounter failure, cut your losses before disaster ensues. And modify immediately your mistakes so you learn.

8. Flexible teams, not departments
Reorganise – try to break down the walls between departments. If you're going to increase your speed, work in small, temporary and flexible teams – and quickly – on key tasks.

9. Product life is shorter than you think
Understanding the life cycle allows you to manage your product or service, to know when to be thinking about phasing out old products and when to phase in new ones without cannibalising existing sales.

10. Speed doesn't kill
Internet marketing is like conventional marketing speeded up. Customers expect replies more quickly, delivery more quickly. Making changes to speed means making changes to working practices. The goal here is to cut dispatch from 28 days down to 2–3 days at the max.

11. Feedback means knowledge – feed-forward means profit
The more you ask, the more competitive advantage you can create, and the stronger your customer relationships become. Then feed-forward, using a twelve-week innovation cycle or a monthly product revision meeting.

12. The 80/20 rule – cut back on rubbish, focus on the juicy bits
If you want to work smarter, focus on the highly effective and ignore the rest! If you can establish a pattern, tap the seam and go after more, similarly profitable customers.

13. Attach the right people to Internet marketing
Assemble a well-balanced team to get the site live, and expect to make changes to the team once it starts to operate. Qualifications for team membership are web-savviness, enthusiasm, customer focus and a desire to change the world.

Create an innovation cycle

Innovation is the core of entrepreneurship. You might describe it as making things better, continually. It's so easy to see it as an attitude – and it's certainly that – but it's much harder to see it as a task. What things do you have to do to innovate?

Most clients I work with will at some stage utter the word 'innovation' in our opening meeting. It'll usually come out with the words 'commitment to' or 'real'. Now, we all aspire to innovation because it's the source of new things, and new is good. And, of course, 'new' is the currency of the Internet, with technology constantly accelerating. It's also the currency of a large part of marketing promotion. But so few companies seem to deliver innovation.

Why? Because most of us lack the framework, the rigour that's necessary to innovate. The world's greatest innovators – the Japanese – are undoubtedly the most systematic people. Innovation is at the front of their minds. I believe passionately that innovation is about doing, not merely having an attitude. It needs a formal dedication to action. A system.

Here's an effective one:

1. Put concrete dates in the diary and divide your innovation cycle into three one-month blocks.
2. The first block should be about gathering ideas – mainly from customers, but also from competitors and staff. Choose the best ones and put the second best on the back burner, perhaps for the next innovation cycle.
3. The second block should be about action – building the ideas so that they can be tested with both staff and customers.
4. The third block should be about completing and polishing the ideas so that they are ready for launch.
5. At the end of your twelve-week cycle, there should be clear evidence that you have listened to your customers and, more importantly, acted on their suggestions.

Here's a simple innovation schedule:

Week 1:   Analyse all customer email feedback for suggestions
Week 2:   Analyse all customer ratings for blackspots in service
Week 3:   Analyse discussion groups for new ideas
Week 4:   Analyse competitor sites, staff favourites for new ideas
Week 5:   Decide which innovations are approved for this cycle
Week 6:   Draft paper prototypes of new innovations
Week 7:   Review paper prototypes

Week 8:   Build innovations
Week 9:   Build innovations
Week 10:   Test innovations on staff and customers
Week 11:   Make revisions
Week 12:   Launch new innovations

Prepare for e-suppliers

Hooking up e-suppliers to your site is probably one of the biggest ways to grow your online business. It opens up opportunities for pricing and choice, branding and delivery that you may previously have only dreamed of.

Let's say you run a complementary-health centre. You're selling services such as massage, reflexology and hypnotism, and you're selling products such as creams, elixirs and books. Your biggest selling product is 'Bella Bundle', a luxury beauty-treatment basket, which is supplied to you by Hardy's Beauty Care. Your e-Commerce site is doing fine, but the paperwork and human activity are starting to mount up:

- You sell fifteen Bella Bundles a day to UK customers, but you can take delivery of only fifty at a time from Hardy's because it's all you have storage space for.
- Your stocks of creams and books fluctuate and, when the supplier is late with deliveries, your web promise of 72-hour delivery is broken.
- You have a treatments diary (effectively an inventory of free treatment rooms and practitioners), which displays availability, but doesn't take bookings. But keeping it online is a troublesome task – it changes every ten minutes or so, and your office has to repost the new diary to the website every time a confirmed booking is made or a practitioner changes their availability.

What can you do to reduce your admin and increase productivity? If you were to hook up your suppliers, it could solve a lot of problems:

- You agree a new contract with Hardy's, securing a 5 per cent discount, your own overbranding on the Basket and direct 24-hour delivery from Hardy's by courier. You set up the site to trigger an email to Hardy's, and to store a record of the order on your database. In one clean sweep, you've just improved customer service, delivery speed, branding, profit margin and eliminated the admin.

- You agree a new contract with your cream and book publishers, in which they use a supplier admin web page on your site to load the delivery dates and product volumes. They can load their own products, pictures and copy, too, under your editorial control. This guarantees

> that availability and dispatch are known quantities to the customer, and encourages the supplier to think of you as a more valuable channel for business. It also hikes your productivity, because you no longer maintain the stock levels manually.
>
> ☐ You database the diary, and have the technology to manage the live publication of the diary to the site. You also set up a booking area for customers and practitioners so that they can update the diary live, thereby cutting out your admin effort. You've just passed control to both customers and suppliers and increased your productivity.

This example shows how easy it is to strengthen your offering and your supplier relations while improving customer relations and value. At no time have you lost control of your brand, your customer or your site.

Of course, you've spent money, but you're a prudent entrepreneur, and you armed yourself with the budgeting planner in Chapter 6.

A brief guide to tax

What are governments doing about sales tax?

In 1999, the Organization for Economic Co-operation and Development (OECD) set out five key principles for national governments to adhere to when taxing transactions. These are:

1. Tax should be neutral
Tax on e-Commerce and Internet transactions should be no different from conventional taxation.

2. Tax should be efficient
Businesses should not suffer high costs when calculating or paying their e-Commerce tax.

3. Tax should be clear
Businesses should understand clearly what the tax rules and regulations are, so that there is minimum cause for dispute with the tax office.

4. Tax should be fair
Tax offices should minimise the opportunities for tax evasion, but should punish evaders on a basis that is proportional to the error.

5. Tax should be flexible
National tax systems should be capable of changing with the innovations and technologies of the immediate and medium-term future.

Where are the official VAT guidelines?

Charging sales tax – VAT in the UK – is still a very green and unclear subject. The VAT office (HM Customs and Excise) has yet to produce a simple set of guidelines that navigate any business through the complicated subject of tax on e-Commerce transactions.

So what is the VAT office likely to do?

At the time of writing, the VAT office had not made it clear how it intended to implement the OECD recommendations. The OECD was not much use either. But many e-Commerce specialists predict that the UK government is likely to press for:

- Digital certificates for every transaction, which identify both the selling and the buying party by name, address and VAT number
- Accurate and tamper-free records of downloaded products as well as records of physically delivered products
- Publication of VAT details (number, registration date) on your website
- Publication of your trading address for every product or service on your website

Is there some kind of taxation standard?

The Internet Engineering Task Force, which controls and sets all standards on the Internet, now supports the Open Trading Protocol (OTP). It's not yet compulsory. But the UK VAT office favours the standard. It simply sets out rules and guidelines on how to keep accurate and tamper-free records of all transactions and downloads for tax purposes. Check out the OTP for yourself at www.otp.org.

So what?

You've created a first draft sustainable development programme. And that's going to ensure a long shelf life for your site. More importantly, you've thought about it before you've built your site. So you're starting to think ahead – a critical activity for successful e-Commerce.

Chapter checklist

Do I have the following?

- [ ] A tracking system that takes account of real-world effects
- [ ] A system of corrective action
- [ ] A flexible innovation cycle
- [ ] A supplier management system
- [ ] A plan for dealing with tax

CHAPTER THIRTEEN

Case studies

The following case studies are based on real companies. Because I want to explore not just the commercial aspects but also the people aspects, I've changed quite a few critical details in each one so they can't be identified. The details I've most frequently changed are industry, names and market conditions. I've tried to leave the challenges, teams and people as real as possible, warts and all!

I've also tried to stick as closely as possible to the framework in this book, but in the real world, that's not always possible. So, where the framework hasn't suited the particulars of a case, I've simply modified it – as you will probably have to.

If you recognise any condition or event in here, think about what makes it familiar to your situation. And, if you don't recognise anything at all, email me with your story or commercial problem – I'm already preparing for my next book! You can reach me at tim@hello-business.com.

Architect, £9,000 budget

This case study is based on a sleepy but capable company, which has just seen the Internet light, and intends to use it as a catalyst for change.

The enterprise

Company:	Dawson's Ltd
Business activity:	Architect
Employees:	30
Turnover:	£1.9m
Serving:	B2B in Birmingham markets
Key customers:	Schools, public housing and offices
Years trading:	22 years

CASE STUDIES

The challenge

The big idea:	Revitalise the business by strengthening field sales and increase value to clients through a feature-rich extranet. The company would also like a superb new image and a new PR programme
The problem:	Low and diminishing sales, declining morale
Chosen site type:	Office (*see* Chapter 8)
Project manager:	Jay, managing director, works four days a week and is not a regular Internet surfer

The starting point

Jay is the founder and MD of a well-established firm of architects. For a while, he's been worrying about the gradual collapse in sales. He has asked his senior partners to a midweek dinner, in town. He wants a frank and informal discussion on where the company is headed, and he wants ideas on reversing the declining sales prospects, which look poor in both the short term and the long term. He's thinking the Internet is the solution.

Two of the senior partners are enthusiastic about changing the sales process, while the other two are sceptical of the Internet. They agree that they have poor sales skills, and that the sales-lead pool is too small and of inadequate quality. They conclude dinner with a brief conversation about image. The company's image is perhaps too old-fashioned, too 'home-made'. They all favour a facelift and a serious step towards contemporary design.

Current market position

The company has no real idea of its competitive market position. It regards most of its competitors as similar. In reality, the cautiousness of architects and the understated, dry image of virtually every competitor means it would be easy for Dawson's to occupy a differentiated, strong position, just by having anything more than a reputation!

Competitors

Jay asks the senior partners and some of the younger architects to surf around. In one afternoon, they find over 35 competitor sites in the UK. They're all brochure sites. Lots of case studies, lots of very large images of buildings, which take a long time to download, and lots of long, laborious descriptions of projects.

Several competitors seem to have private 'clients only' areas. Surprisingly, perhaps, most sites have a boring, undesigned look about them.

Available resources

Money is tight, and so is time. Up to 30 per cent of partners' time is taken up with free feasibility studies. This makes selling very costly (to combat this, Dawson's often reject projects they think they can't win, using educated guesswork).

So Jay is thinking that a £3,000 budget is about as much as can be spent. And that a new logo will have to be designed in-house. He contacts a few e-Commerce agencies and listens to their ideas. After a few weeks (and a few budget shocks!) he settles on an agency that proposes a hybrid offline/online project, with a focus on sales productivity. Perhaps he also chooses the people he likes best.

Suitability check

The agency does a quick analysis of the company suitability to the Internet, using the diagram from Chapter 2.

Jay is getting more interested. But his enthusiasm rises when the agency starts talking about improving the sales process, without using major surgery on the website.

The approach

Here's the project broken down into chunks.

Building the team

Jay assembles a web team that has a sales bias. This is a wise decision, as it's more likely to generate popular support among senior staff. He appoints the following:

- the contract manager as 'floor manager'
- a young recently recruited architect who's been pretty vocal about the Internet as 'maverick'
- the finance director to act as the money controller
- an old and very supportive client to advise on service
- an engineering consultant from an engineering firm they frequently collaborate with to advise on extranet
- the e-Commerce agency as 'adviser'
- himself as the chair and 'detective'

The project has started. Jay hosts a first meeting with the e-Commerce agency to map out the project. They agree on a combined offline/online project – a website with a marketing programme.

Then Jay holds a second meeting at 5 p.m. the same day to brief all staff on the forthcoming project. The overall reaction from staff is cautious enthusiasm. Some of them were unaware of the tricky sales position.

Choosing the model

The agency suggests the Office model as the basis for their site (*see* Chapter 8). They sketch out on a single sheet of A4 a brochure site that ties in closely to a rigorous new sales process, with a security-protected extranet for project documents such as drawings, specifications and computer images. They agree that the new image on the site must be reflected in the new printed sales literature. Team enthusiasm is rising!

Doing the research

The web team review the 35 competitor sites again, this time listing functions and buttons they could adapt for use on their own site. Clearly the site focus is going to be on content (mainly case studies), not whizzy buttons.

Segmenting the market

The team review their existing market segments and agree there's no reason to change them, each having equal priority.

- Schools in the Birmingham area
- Public housing in the Birmingham and surrounding area
- Offices in the Birmingham area

They have always avoided work (and sales prospects) outside the Birmingham area because transport time and costs cut their competing power. The agency suggests this needs reconsideration, because the website is available to everyone in the UK.

Selecting the right strategies

The web team meet to address market issues and some of their own 'political' issues, and agree on five key strategies. Here's an extract from their strategy paper:

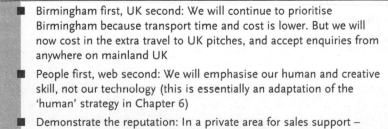

- Birmingham first, UK second: We will continue to prioritise Birmingham because transport time and cost is lower. But we will now cost in the extra travel to UK pitches, and accept enquiries from anywhere on mainland UK
- People first, web second: We will emphasise our human and creative skill, not our technology (this is essentially an adaptation of the 'human' strategy in Chapter 6)
- Demonstrate the reputation: In a private area for sales support – showing more commercially sensitive information such as fee rates,

- current live projects and guides for clients on preparing tender documents
- Rigour in sales: A ten-step sales process will front an effective and thorough offline system, which will be supplemented by the private sales-support area
- Extranet rigour: We will load all our drawings and project documents to the extranet on time, and use it as our master project host

Competitive strategies

The team is running on a low budget in an undifferentiated market. Most competitors have case-study-driven brochure sites and low sales skills. So the team decides that the appropriate competitive strategies are:

- Diplomatic nous: Forging functional and content links with consulting engineers, schools organisations and public housing bodies
- Mild mobile defence: Keeping the innovation on the site just a little further ahead of the competition, backed with good case-study publicity

Setting targets

Next they set targets for the combined site and marketing programme.

- ☐ Win in first six months £0.3m in new business fees (this is to exclude all leads currently in the pipeline)
- ☐ Close one in four of all existing leads within first six months
- ☐ Increase sales productivity by 20 per cent – measured in man days per win
- ☐ 20 per cent net profit resulting from those online sales

Setting the budget

The £3k budget is clearly too small. But the goals are now much higher. Using a profit-to-cost ratio of 3:1 (six months is a very short time for pay-back), they should allow a budget of 20 per cent × £0.3m ÷ 5 = £12k. But money is too tight. They agree to raise the budget to £9k, which includes the initial consultancy costs.

The e-Commerce agency builds the site in ten days. Initial client feedback is very positive.

Creating people processes

This was one of the biggest areas of value in the project. The agency created a ten-step sales process for Dawson's.

To underpin the sales process, the agency recommended simple hidden devices that could be revealed by salespeople at significant moments. Jay liked the approach – its theatricality lifted their sales style out of the usual architectural stuffy understatement.

Step	Goal	Offline work	Online tool
1	Establish contact	Send postcard, letter or pack promoting a specific web page depending on segment or size of client	Specific case study and marketing brochure pages for specific segments and targets
2	Secure meeting	Follow-up call for meeting	Reveal confidential online case studies that are appropriate to client (1 from 40)
3	Demo skills and systems	Present credentials and abilities	Demo the extranet
4	Pitch for feasibility study	Suggest a lightweight or paid-for feasibility study	Reveal template feasibility study on web
5	Conduct feasibility study	Conduct study	Post results on web
6	Help draft tender	Suggest client use a tender draft	Reveal online tender document
7	Submit proposal	Write and submit proposal document, responding to tender	Publish a simple web summary of the proposal document
8	Present proposal	Pitch meeting	Use specific online case studies to illustrate pitch
9	Negotiate profitable terms	Commercial negotiation meeting	Online fun tool demonstrates how to set a budget without compromising quality
10	Sign agreement	Agreement signed	PR released on site

Unexpected problems

1. The web team had not appreciated the sheer volume of copy writing to get forty case studies prepared. So they decided to release twenty for launch and then three (one from each segment) every month.

2. Drafting a new sales proposal document caused considerable team dissent – half the team thought it was 'too slick' even to submit proposals instead of simply responding to tender documents. It was agreed to assess each pitch on a one-off basis.
3. Living the new sales system was tricky, too. Staff were reluctant to adjust the way they sold. But gradually, over six months, most came round.

The results

The practice had a simple but well-designed site – a combination of brochure and extranet – and after six months had achieved superb results:

- £0.4m in new fees (excluding leads previously in the pipeline)
- closed one in three of all existing leads
- increased sales productivity by 28 per cent – measured in man days per win
- 11 per cent net profit resulting from those new sales

Their only disappointment was net profit. Their commercial negotiation was letting them down – and that was the focus of their next marketing project.

Data communications agency, £225,000 budget

This case study is based on an ambitious partnership, which seeks to dominate a new market within 2 years.

The enterprise

Company:	WowCom Ltd
Business activity:	Data communications agency, offering a choice of datalines
Employees:	5
Turnover:	£1.8m
Serving:	B2B in UK, then English-speaking markets
Key customers:	Small Office, Home Office (SoHo), Small business
Years trading:	Start-up

The challenge

The big idea:	Offer small businesses a choice of datalines, and remove the complexity of comparing. The company wants to be first into the UK market, then move to English-speaking markets
The problem:	No investment funds yet, just a five-page business plan. Starting up quickly before large telephone companies (telcos) enter the market
Chosen site type:	Market Portal (*see* Chapter 8)
Project manager:	Martha, co-founder, can apply 50 per cent of her time to the project

The starting point

Martha and Phil are sitting at the kitchen table, papers, books and magazines strewn all over the room. They are both huddled over a laptop, where Martha is putting the finishing touches to her five-page start-up business plan. Phil has taken a half-day off from the office in order to be here for this meeting.

Martha runs her own small telecom installation company and Phil works for a small telecoms brokerage. Together, they've hatched an idea for an online dataline agency that will be based in the UK. Datalines transmit computer data from one place to another. The idea is to build a centre where companies can shop for and compare datalines from any of the major telcos. It's a kind of dataline warehouse.

Phil has pulled together good statistics from industry sources, and has created two-year forecasts of consumer and business trends. He has also built a simple cash-flow forecast. Martha, on the other hand, has been drafting strategies and resources for the new business. After today's session, they plan to show their outline business idea to a few trusted colleagues and friends who will give them objective feedback.

Current market position
Currently, of course, there is no market position. This is a start-up business. The entrepreneurs have an idea that price is the best market position to take – in other words, being known for cutting dataline prices – and have drafted this into their plan.

Competitors
They've been surfing for days and, to their astonishment, found no online competition. In the UK, there are a growing number of telecom brokers, all of whom offer consultancy or procurement services, but none

of them offer a dataline warehouse. In the USA, there are more advanced sites and certainly more brokers. But all the brokers focus on punishing the telco. Martha and Phil's idea is to serve the telco by bringing their products to the market.

Available resources

There are, of course, no resources yet. They're well connected – they're both currently in the business and can recruit good people directly without paying fees.

The entrepreneurs have a little money of their own, but not enough even to pay web designers or e-Commerce consultants to make a start on the site. They need finance and fast.

The approach

Here's the project broken down into chunks.

Building the team

The entrepreneurs call in an e-Commerce consultant at this stage, and ask him for his views on the business plan and what the project would involve.

The consultant suggests that, before any work starts, they make a comprehensive overhaul of the business plan to give it credibility. He also suggests a revenue model and that they prioritise the search for investors by developing a knockout investor pack – the whole project is going to be delayed without it.

Because there are insufficient funds, the new three-person team agree to cover all the roles required between them – Martha will be chair, customer and detective, Phil will be financial controller and floor manager and the consultant will be adviser and maverick. Work starts right away.

Choosing the model

Originally, the entrepreneurs had envisaged a Shop model (*see* Chapter 8). Customers would come into a simple comparison web page where they could search for the dataline package of their choice. But what if a competitor were to copycat the site? Especially if it was an existing offline specialist. With good expertise and experience, they would surely be able to match or beat WowCom prices.

Perhaps the original idea could be improved on. Brokers' businesses are usually based on price or personal contacts. That's fine in the offline world, but hardly sustainable here. The team decide on a stronger, harder-to-beat approach: woo the telcos as well as the end users. Create a marketplace where choice and value are the drivers, not just price, where matching your needs to just the right dataline package offers more value than even a 10 per cent saving, and where telcos will be able to retain more profit. The Market Portal model offers just that.

Doing the research

The consultant conducts a mini-survey on twenty small businesses and twenty telcos, revealing a strong interest in the entrepreneurs' ideas. Together with two major industry reports on business expectations in datalines over the next five years, the market picture is complete: customer expectations are running high, choice is too complex, there's no one-stop shop to buy from because competition is not firmly established. In other words, customers are all hyped up with nowhere to go. It seems they're on to a winner. Martha's earlier research is revisited, but there's still no sign of a major UK competitor. 'It looks like we're going to be first into the market,' says Martha in disbelief.

Segmenting the market

In the business plan, the entrepreneurs had identified two main market segments – small businesses and big businesses. From the industry reports they have, it's clear there are two other segments – micro-businesses and consumers. Here's the segmentation the team agrees:

- Consumer (likely to need single line)
- Micro or SoHo business (likely to seek single or twin lines)
- Small business (likely to need up to 25 lines and other services)
- Large business (25 lines or over, and multiple services)

Selecting the right strategies

Martha understands that strategy is long-term thinking, stuffed into catchphrases. She sets out her thinking in an email to Phil.

To:	Phil
From:	Martha
Subject:	Strategy

Hi, Phil.

I've been drafting up ideas for strategy: Any thoughts?

Strategy 1 – Suppliers first, buyers second

We must recruit at least 50 telcos to be sure of offering choice before we launch. If the cupboard's bare, no one will shop.

Strategy 2 – Functionality not price

We should push our site's power and interactivity to the maximum. Obviously, we want decent discounts, but everyone's going to be in the cutthroat game – we need to stay above it.

Strategy 3 – Multinational as fast as possible

The benefits of cutting good deals with overseas telcos are high. So let's get into the US and Europe as quickly as we can afford.

What do you think?

Cheers, Martha.

Phil agrees. They meet with their consultant to formulate a start-up strategy. They choose 'integration strategy' – high on both customer focus and engaging features, resulting in loyalty and a real buzz. They're clearly going to need a high human presence to support this enterprise – but they suspected that anyway. A lot of staff will be required for supplier management and customer account management.

Competitive strategies
This is trickier than it seems. The entrepreneurs initially believe that the best approach is 'David v. Goliath' – have a go at the big boys. But there aren't any! There's really no one in this marketplace yet – they may be Goliath themselves in a few months' time!

Here, the team agree to wait and see. This doesn't mean do nothing, of course: it means preparing a range of responses to competitor attack, such as dynamic pricing, withdrawal from selective market segments, innovation and stronger targeting. But they'll decide on that later.

Setting targets and a budget

Martha and Phil work through a detailed revenue model with the consultant and fix realistic relationships between costs and revenues. The key relationships are 1 service staff member per 350 small customers and 1 per 100 large customers. They also set a ratio of £1 marketing spend per £7.50 revenue. This focuses their finances on productivity and leads them to the following targets:

- ☐ Online sales worth £1.8m within 12 months
- ☐ One online repeat customer per 3.5 first-time customers
- ☐ Two hundred telcos signed up within twelve months
- ☐ Break even within twelve months
- ☐ One overseas office open within twelve months

They set their budgets as follows:

Item	Cost	Your Input
Commercial Planning		
Revenue Model Consultancy	£4,000	6 days
Brief Business Plan Consultancy	£2,500	3 days
Investor Preparation Consultancy	£2,500	5 days
Total	£9,000	
Architecture		
Structure & Page Maps Workshops & Design	£16,000	7 days
Functionality List Workshops & Design	£8,000	5 days
Total	£24,000	
Production		
Visual Design Fees	£9,000	4 days
Software Coding Fees	£173,000	Nil
Total	£182,000	
Implementation		
Hosting & Domain	£5,000	Nil
Software Licences	£5,000	Nil
Total	£10,000	
Grand Total	£225,000	
Maintenance		
Technical Support	£2,000 pm	Nil
Content Support	£2,500 pm	2 day pm
Total	£4,500 pm	

This budget demonstrates a commitment to powerful functionality, dynamic pricing and profitability.

Creating people processes

From the business model, it's clear the company will depend on three key people processes:

- [ ] Recruiting telcos – this is a sales-and-account-management function, which is critical to choice of service. Staff will need good sales material, a good demonstration of how the system works for telcos and good legal contracts.

- [ ] Swapping customer dataline accounts – this is a laborious system, in which staff will open new, better, cheaper telco accounts on behalf of customers, and close their old ones down for them. They will have to use telco paperwork for this.

- [ ] Negotiating with telcos and affiliates – this is a human-relationship process, which should produce better prices and better promotions on a continual improvement basis.

Good staff and supporting materials are required to make these processes go with a swing.

After initial seedcorn funding is secured, the consultant's company designs and builds the site in ten weeks. Martha and Phil are involved in every step of the design and architecture work.

Unexpected problems

Martha had not appreciated how much work was involved in recruiting telcos. At first they were very enthusiastic. As soon as the contracts and commercial negotiation appeared, they all wanted far more documentation and meetings than anticipated. In fact she succeeded in securing only thirty telcos by launch, but, once her staff were hired, she gradually built that to 145 over the year.

Phil had not appreciated how much time he needed to inject into the project and this slowed the early development considerably. Because he was the dataline expert, his input was critical to the initial planning work. He kept his full-time job at the brokerage right up until the site went live, before moving to join the company full-time. As a result, the project start was delayed by nearly three months.

Recruitment was harder than expected, too. The entrepreneurs assumed (as they often do) that people of their own calibre were readily available on the market. This was not the case, and Martha and Phil had to wear twice as many hats as they had planned during the first nine months of the company's life.

The results

After twelve months, the results were looking good:

- online sales or orders worth £1.6m
- one online repeat customer per 7.5 first-time customers

- 145 telcos signed up within twelve months
- profit of 1.2 per cent achieved in first year of trading
- one overseas office open

Generally, the team – and their investors – were happy with the results. But they were a little disappointed with the market response. Clearly, some customers and telcos weren't sharing their enthusiasm for this new way of trading. The buzz effect they were hoping for among their customer community was a little low. Better customer education was required. Their promotional work was cut out for Year 2.

Office equipment distributor, £85,000 budget

This case study is based on an old-fashioned company modernising the hard way. Conflicting attitudes to risk within the management team were eventually overcome.

The enterprise

Company:	EB Office Equipment plc
Business activity:	Office equipment dealer, offering a combined catalogue and tailor-made service
Employees:	125
Turnover:	£11m
Serving:	B2B in UK markets
Key customers:	Dealers, large companies, small companies
Years trading:	44

The challenge

The big idea:	Conquer the market, widen the supplier base and become the de facto source for anything to do with modern office equipment. The company would also like to see more profit from equipment sales and a better, higher profile image
The problem:	Declining profits, increasing dependency on low-margin products, management team bad communicators
Chosen site type:	Shop model (see Chapter 8)
Project manager:	Jo, marketing manager, reporting to the board, overwhelmed with workload

The starting point

It's late Friday afternoon, and the directors have finally agreed to meet up with Jo, the marketing manager, to discuss the website. She's got a head full of ideas and buckets of enthusiasm for e-Commerce. She's prepared a punchy presentation, which sets out the case for a £100,000 investment spread over two years.

The boardroom is stuffed with trophies and beautiful, antique products which chart the company's 44 years in the business. The directors are proud of the company's track record since World War Two, and often relate the story to prospective clients of how they were two steps ahead of everyone else when manual typewriters were in demand.

In the last twenty years, the company has successfully introduced a massive range of office equipment – from staplers to pencil sharpeners and from sticky notes to clocks. And, since the early 1990s, they have supplemented these products with a range of computer accessories, which they manufacture themselves. This includes screen guards, monitor stands and keyboard dust covers.

The old range is highly profitable, but the competition in the marketplace for computer accessories has become fierce, and very price-driven. The company sells mainly through dealers. Indeed 90 per cent of sales come from this source. The remaining 10 per cent come from established clients in the form of direct sales.

Jo moves professionally through the presentation, highlighting all the key benefits, risks and opportunities, pausing to explain how the Internet will impact on not just their business but the entire industry. She backs up her argument with a few choice statistics.

The directors are impressed, but not moved to action. They understand the arguments, but still see the Internet as a wait-and-see option (they are regular users of email and use their PCs on a daily basis). After some discussion, uncertainties arise. They ask Jo to explore how she can achieve twice the results on half the budget.

Current market position

Before the meeting, when Jo sat down to analyse the company's competitive position, she couldn't find a clear or consistent view among her biggest clients. They seemed vague about what made the company different and no one said it was unique.

However, Jo could at least tell the board that the company was recognised by its dealer network as market leader for computer accessories. Track record and experience were usually cited as the main reasons for their leadership. And yet this was their lowest-margin-product family.

By contrast, Jo found the company to be an 'also-ran' in other product ranges. It seemed as though the lower their reputation was, the higher was their profit – and vice versa!

Competitors

Here is the competitive analysis that Jo presented in the first board meeting. As we can see, the competition is varied. In the computer accessories market, the company's up against price competition from a number of young businesses (the price differentials are tiny). In the office equipment market, the opposition is mature and well established (there's a greater diversity of competing factors).

Computer Accessories

	Design	Functionality (incl payment)	Catalogue Choice	Product Quality	Price	Value
Average	100%	100%	100%	100%	100%	100%
Dolcom	90%	105%	80%	86%	101%	66%
Briers	75%	100%	120%	100%	99%	89%
Screenstuff	85%	105%	110%	114%	100%	112%
Us	110%	110%	110%	100%	100%	133%

General Office Equipment

	Design	Functionality (incl payment)	Catalogue Choice	Product Quality	Price	Value
Average	100%	100%	100%	100%	100%	100%
Bannister	109%	87%	124%	90%	104%	110%
Briers	75%	114%	108%	100%	93%	86%
Go Office	75%	107%	115%	88%	101%	82%
Us	110%	110%	110%	100%	100%	133%

Clearly, the EB opportunities for competitive value are good. Jo's 'us' figures above are her proposed targets not the actual scores.

Available resources

The company doesn't have deep pockets. The profit figures are way down in the low single figures, and, although cash flow is very healthy, a commitment on the £100k scale that Jo's after is going to meet with a 'no'. Either more cash is going to have to be sourced, or the project's going to be a lot smaller.

The company also doesn't have any web or e-Commerce skills, and there's no experience even in Jo's mind on how the Internet works. Everyone at manager level or above is overworked.

There is a little online history, though – twelve months previously, the company paid a web designer £3,000 to build an online brochure. Reaction from dealers was mixed – those that hadn't seen it were impressed that they had a site, and those that had seen it were not impressed with the amateur design, flashing pictures and overtly exaggerated sales claims. The site was duly withdrawn, which prompted Jo to look more closely at e-Commerce.

Suitability check

Jo is determined to present a stronger case back to the board, and asks an e-Commerce consultant to help her build a rock-solid presentation.

First, they turn their attention to the suitability of the product and service to the Internet. All products can easily be catalogued. A good score here.

Second, they examine the business suitability, using the business suitability table from Chapter 2.

Issue	Significance	Score	Weighted Score
Part of our product can be downloaded	0	0	0
Part of our product can be catalogued	10	10	100
Our product is easily delivered to the door	10	10	100
The net will not dilute our personal service	10	8	80
Growing % of customers are online	6	8	48
We have clear-cut work systems	10	3	30
Our competitors are trading online	10	2	20
Our management team is online	6	2	12
Our suppliers are online	3	5	15
Total	65	48	405
% Score			62.3%

Again a good score here. But probably some improvement in management commitment and competitor-catching are going to be needed.

Third, they discreetly examine management suitability, including the board's! The consultant describes the management as 'a curious mixture of good delegation and bad communication'. There's a love of short-term money, and a fear of long-term planning and change. This looks like a major hurdle to overcome throughout the project.

Jo works with the consultant to beef up the argument to proceed. Here are the key points of their case:

- We must raise profits through productivity from online transactions
- We're not behind the competition – yet
- We could help modernise our dealer network, which would improve relations
- Let's lead this marketplace, not just play in it!

Without raising the issues of management skills or cash, Jo and the consultant secured approval to proceed with a 'major e-Commerce programme', and accepted that the budget would be agreed (and would probably be smaller than necessary) when more information was available. Now the project could begin.

The approach

Building the team

Jo asks the managing director to chair the team. Smart move: this gives him a sense of control, will help to bring him up to speed on the Internet and he'll have to hear the full arguments (repeatedly) for investment. It also gives him an extra diary burden!

She suggests and assembles a team consisting of a head of operations to act as 'floor-manager', a rebellious web monkey who works in marketing as 'maverick', the finance director to act as the money policeman, a web-savvy customer to champion the service corner, the e-Commerce consultant as 'adviser' and herself as the 'detective'. The meter is now running.

The MD hosts a first meeting to brief all other senior and management level staff on the forthcoming project. He's showered with more questions than he can answer, but the consultant deals with them. The word is out now. The MD agrees to keep on top of the rumour mill, and to host bi-weekly briefing sessions for all senior staff. They're reasonably reassured.

Choosing the model

Jo creates a comprehensive revenue model, with the help of the consultant. They weigh up all the possibilities and, after adding in real-world effects such as seasonality and competitor reaction, they settle on a first-year target of £0.75m in sales and 10 per cent net profit resulting from those online sales. This should really be higher, but they're erring on the side of caution.

Next they consider the business model. Jo wants to sell goods from multiple suppliers and continue to grow that supplier base. She also wants to grow the dealer network (her customers) and possibly prepare for a direct-selling operation in a year's time. The simplest model that fits here is the shop model (*see* Chapter 8) with a syndication service added in. The consultant suggests they phase in some of the more advanced and costly functionality after the site has washed its face financially.

Doing the research

The maverick now comes into his own, and presents a list of 22 drop-dead sites. Jo sensitively weeds out the wild ones, and asks him to compile a list of functions that would work well on the new site – even add his own ideas if he likes.

Meanwhile, the consultant is devising a customer survey, which Jo's team can conduct in a two-day burst. It's designed to gather basic information on customer attitudes towards online purchasing and to identify any possible 'vertical audiences' – potential specialist areas for online communities, such as ergonomics, presentation techniques and group buying.

The survey results are encouraging. Most dealers are already online, and have nowhere to shop easily online. They can place orders direct with some manufacturers, but there's no one single shop where they can compare. The vertical audience research draws a bit of a blank. The consultant suggests a review of the situation in six months, when they may need to harness greater community loyalty under more competitive conditions.

Segmenting the market

Although Jo's pretty clear on which marketing segments she's targeting for this year, the consultant helps her run a segment checklist over them, and they identify the following priorities:

- Dealers – high
- Direct to companies – high
- Direct to schools and universities – medium
- Direct to hotels – low

But this would put a different spin on the site. Jo had originally envisaged a site for dealers only. Now, she's worried that the dealers (and the directors!) may resist selling direct, because it may damage relations with – and sales from – dealers. It's the old 'cutting-out-the-middleman' problem.

They load the proposed segments back into the revenue model, and mess around with the options – hostile dealer reaction, low take-up from the direct market and so on. The results don't help much. The possible hostility could seriously damage business, but a successful direct campaign could double sales. A clever solution is required.

Selecting the right strategies

The web team meet in the MD's office for a brainstormer. They use all the walls and windows for posting up notes and diagrams. The consultant hosts the workshop, and helps to keep the mood creative. After nearly six hours and ample supplies of coffee, cola and sandwiches, they arrive at a solution:

1. Protect existing dealer business by offering a syndicated service to them. The company will offer a custom version of its website to dealers, which can be overbranded, using the dealer's colours, logo and own brochure copy. The dealers (many of whom cannot afford a major website) will get huge value. They'll also be tied in more closely to EB. And the company can make a small profit on the service.

2. Ramp up customer service. There's a debate over what standard of telesales or telesupport is appropriate, and whether a bit of good old-fashioned sparkle needs to be injected to the current team. Everyone agrees they'll need email tools to make confirmations of order, processing, dispatch and follow-up as productive as possible.

3. Build the reputation. The team are united on what must happen here. They're striking out into a leading position in their industry, and must build their reputation quickly, probably using PR and trade-press advertising. The particular points they choose to emphasise are the ones that will make it harder for competitors to follow: personal service, superb functionality, huge product choice, excellent value. With PR, they'll have to tell stories that emphasise these points.

4. Speed up order processing. The company will have to find a way of dispatching goods in 24 hours. They identify two current bottlenecks that need eliminating: credit clearance and physical packaging. It's suggested that they sign a deal with FedEx or UBS.

5. 'Integration strategy', pursuing a balance of good site and good human service.

The biggest part of the session was a debate over whether to pursue 'automation strategy' (with its emphasis on technology and low human intervention) or 'integration strategy' (with its emphasis on balance). Automation appealed to the operations people because they liked the idea of technology handling most of the petty and admin-intensive enquiries. But, when the team figured through the risks of weakened relations with dealers during a tricky first year of e-Commerce, it was agreed that 'integration strategy' was appropriate.

Competitive strategies

As around four competitors already had sites ahead of EB – albeit low-quality ones – Jo worked with the consultant on competitive strategy. They knew they were arriving late in a low-level e-Commerce market, so they had the advantage of understanding competitor mistakes and the advantage of surprise. The strategies they selected were:

- Blocking attack, closing out competitors from dealers. They chose to broaden their product range to supply everything that dealers needed, thereby cutting out the need to go to competitors.
- Diplomatic nous, aiming to tie in dealers on an exclusive basis. This would involve a large dealer-account management campaign.

Setting targets

The following first-draft targets are set:

- [ ] Online sales from existing dealers worth £500k within six months
- [ ] Online sales from new dealers worth £300k within six months
- [ ] A hundred dealers buying the syndicated service within twelve months
- [ ] Online sales from direct customers worth £250k within twelve months
- [ ] Profit of 20 per cent from all online sales

Setting the budget

After the targets are agreed, the budget is calculated. They've set mainly six-month targets, so they'll go with a 3:1 return ratio. This implies £900k × 20 per cent ÷ 3 = £60k. The consultant suggests this is too small for their intended functionality – around £80k would seem more appropriate. The FD concedes, but with the proviso that over twelve months the profit payback is 6:1 (the FD drives a hard bargain!). The project scope implies the following investment is required:

Item	Cost	Jo's Input
Commercial Planning		
Revenue & Pricing Model Consultancy	£5,000	3 days
Total	£5,000	
Architecture		
Structure & Page Maps Workshops & Design	£7,000	3 days
Functionality List Workshops & Design	£3,000	1 day
Total	£10,000	
Production		
Visual Design Fees	£6,500	2 days
Software Coding Fees	£59,500	Nil
Total	£66,000	

Item	Cost	Jo's Input
Implementation		
Hosting & Domain	£1,500	Nil
Software Licences	£2,500	Nil
Total	£4,000	
Grand Total	£85,000	
Maintenance		
Technical Support	£1,500 pm	Nil
Content Support	£1,000 pm	Half day pm
Total	£2,500 pm	

Creating people processes

The MD hires a telesales telesupport trainer for a three-day training programme for all telesales staff, to inject personality, professionalism and charm to the team's somewhat blunt style.

The e-Commerce consultant designs simple email tools for semi-automated confirmations for processing, dispatch and follow-up.

A new accounts person is hired to speed up processing time for credit clearance. Her first quarter targets are set at 70 per cent of all morning orders to be cleared before 1 p.m. on the same day. A new online credit-clearance service is secured with a European specialist.

The warehouse is reorganised for same-day selection and packing. One new manager is hired to champion the customer, and is given a first-quarter target of getting 60 per cent of orders dispatched on the same day, and the other 40 per cent the next day. A deal is signed with UPS.

The site is built in nine weeks, with Jo and the MD keeping a close involvement throughout.

The results

The project is a huge success. Jo reported these figures after just five months:

- online sales from existing customers worth £600k
- online sales from new customers worth £380k
- 65 dealers buying the syndicated service
- online sales from direct customers worth £230k

The site had wildly exceeded targets. Jo was now in a position to bid for further finance to expand the site's development.

▮ Record distributor, £25,000 budget

This case study is based on a visionary workaholic, who saw the Internet as a way of increasing productivity and profit as well as competing harder.

The enterprise

Company:	Sniff'n'Scratch Records Ltd
Business activity:	Specialist supplier of vinyl records
Employees:	8
Turnover:	£1.1m
Serving:	B2B and B2C in international markets
Key customers:	DJs, clubs, record stores, consumers
Years trading:	8

The challenge

The big idea:	Increase sales and order productivity, and focus on improving delivery. The company would also like to break into the UK direct-to-consumer market, and create a very trendy 'underground' image
The problem:	Too thinly stretched resources serving fifteen countries from a base in London, and small average order size hurts profit
Chosen site type:	Shop (*see* Chapter 8)
Project manager:	Robbo, managing director, very overworked and a poor delegator

The starting point

Robbo knows his market and his business well. Sniff'n'Scratch is one of the world leaders in a niche market – supplying vinyl to scratch DJs and scratch vinyl stores. They don't deal direct with the consumer.

The business is staffed entirely by knowledgeable, male over-forty-year-olds – no trendies with nose rings here. They have realised that their customers' market is moving online fast, with MPEG and other technologies fuelling consumer demand. They want to get on the gravy train before their competitors gobble up the market share.

Current market position and competitors

There are only six companies worldwide with such a specialism. The company is known for its leading stock of European and Latin American records, while others specialise in soul, rock, reggae, blues and others.

There is no service, price or speed leader, and every player has a music specialism which it jealously guards.

One competitor – Garcy's – has pushed itself online, with a superb-looking site targeted at consumers, not trade.

Available resources

Cash is very tight. Robbo runs a prudent budget and always thinks about payback before anything else. There are good PC skills within his small team. And the obsessive nature of the business means people are used to working long hours (the phone is often manned till midnight to serve the USA market).

The approach

Building the team

No choices here – there's only one person with any time for this project and that's Robbo himself. Robbo is a self-confessed bad delegator and insists that everyone else has to stay full-time on product sourcing, handling customer orders and dispatch. Robbo recruits a good e-Commerce agency to undertake the main part of the work for him, and to act as outsource, consultancy and constructor all rolled into one.

Choosing the model

The agency recommends a Shop business model (*see* Chapter 8). Since the company already has an extensive inventory database, Robbo hopes his workload will be small in moving it online.

The catalogue will be searchable by artist, date, label, music category, composer and the company's cleverly crafted style labels. These include sample (solo instrument, loop, voice, chord), emotional (such as gloomy, pensive, exuberant and optimistic) and aural mood (such as splashy, loose, tight and processed). They categorise many of their records to help their customers find exactly what they're looking for. The company often plays thirty seconds of the music down the phone to customers who want to hear before they buy. Robbo has asked if they can do this on the Internet – it would lighten their load enormously.

Orders will be accepted online from account customers and then invoiced offline (thus keeping the credit arrangements of their existing customers). For non-account customers, a credit card will be accepted.

Research and Segmenting the market

The agency contacts overseas record stores to get feedback on the key features of the proposed site. After the analysis, the agency suggests subdividing the existing market segments:

- DJs – professional
- DJs – semi-pro
- Vinyl stores – specialist
- Vinyl stores – broad

It also suggests some new ones, which Robbo researches:

- CD stores, seeking scratch credibility
- Serious collector
- General consumer

All three new market segments offer good opportunities, provided they can overcome two major obstacles – small order size and differing levels of customer knowledge (experts don't want to be treated like beginners, and vice versa).

Also, the opportunities for hosting a vinyl discussion group are attractive – it's a good vertical community with a known preference for collecting (i.e. spending).

They come up with a bundling system that offers bundles of ten, seven, five and three records at unit prices of £12, £13, £14 and £15 respectively. It also charges a marked-up delivery to cover for single orders.

To address the customer-knowledge problem, they settle on a dual interface, which allows customers to elect themselves as experts or intermediates. The difference is in street language and design.

And they settle on a well-designed vinyl discussion group, which will remain uncensored and undergroundy.

Selecting the right transition and competitive strategies

The agency hosts a major strategy work session, where Robbo agrees to the following strategies:

- ☐ Improve service and delivery: Increasing the telesales cover to 24 hours, launching a dual delivery promotion for offline and online business (48-hour delivery online, 48-hour offline to reassure offline customers)
- ☐ Protect existing custom: Guarantee of Internet prices to offline customers, publishing the telesales hotline on the website and basing their order system on the new website

☐ Flanking attack: Using the thirty-second sample and special search words and to achieve an early, conclusive victory. This is aimed specifically at Garcy's, his only online competitor

☐ Niche defence: Seeking to dominate the market in European and Latin American vinyl by offering a finder service guaranteeing to locate any record within fourteen days or give money back. This is also aimed at his major competitors

Setting targets

Next they set targets for the combined site and marketing programme.

☐ Win in first twelve months £300k in online business from new customers

☐ Win in first twelve months £300k in online business from existing customers

☐ Increase productivity by 50 per cent – measured in man-days per sales £

☐ Increase company net profit to 15 per cent

Setting the budget

With these targets, the business is forecasting sales of £1.4m and profit of £210k. That's £125k bigger than last year's profit of £85k. Robbo figures there should be a 5:1 payback ratio and so sets his budget at £25k.

Creating people processes

The agency suggests a few changes to people processes:

☐ Contract with an international courier such as FedEx or UPS

☐ Bigger catalogues to support the Blocking attack strategy

☐ One member of staff to take full – delegated responsibility for the site

☐ Changes to stationery, packaging and dispatch notes

The site is designed and built by the agency in seven weeks, with Robbo keeping a regular eye on its development.

The results

Robbo is well on course for success on the sales front. At Month 4, he achieves his six-month targets. His launch was well received by press and customers alike. Unfortunately, several unexpected problems arose:

- CD stores seeking scratch credibility amounted to nothing. Robbo could not interest them in vinyl at all.

- Serious collectors were very interested in the site but reluctant to buy in fives or tens. The Amazon effect (cheap books, one by one) was keeping sales productivity low. Higher prices were the only answer.

- General consumers were visiting, but not buying. They filled the discussion group with dumb questions which the expert customers hated. So Robbo created a new discussion group for customers only.

Packaging wholesaler, £160,000 budget

This case study is based on an entrepreneurial partnership, who lacked quite a bit of Internet knowledge, but made up for it in market knowledge.

The enterprise

Company:	AllPack Ltd
Business activity:	Packaging services
Employees:	10
Turnover:	£2.0m target
Serving:	B2B in UK urban markets
Key customers:	Businesses of all sizes, packaging specialists
Years trading:	Start-up

The challenge

The big idea:	Corner the market in B2B packaging. The goal is to create real customer focus, and quickly penetrate the UK market and then European markets
The problem:	No investment funds, entrepreneurs' ambitions far outstrip their resources, already some good competitors in the marketplace
Chosen site type:	A variant of the Market Portal model (see Chapter 8)
Project manager:	Helen, co-founder, can apply 50 per cent of her time to the project

The starting point

Helen is meeting her first potential investors today. It's a wet April Thursday morning, and she's presenting her business plan. It took two months to research and write and today is its first real test. She's nervous.

Helen's idea is to create a business that is both broad and deep. That is, an enterprise that serves any customer with any packaging-related need, down to every last detail. Boxes, card, plastics, ink, finishing, protective materials, printing, graphics, distribution, anything! There are at least six separate product groups. It's a monster. It's a monopoly.

The capitalists politely shred her plan. The finances look solid, they say, but there's no evidence of decent marketing or competitive advantage. They ask her penetrating questions about the quality of management and the scale of her business that she can't answer. The investors are sharper and more business-savvy than Helen had expected. Dispirited, she reviews her plan.

Current market position and competitors
Perhaps the capitalists are right. If there's no differentiation or competitive bite in Helen's plan, there's no business. Perhaps she has approached things too theoretically. Perhaps the plan lacks heart, marketing realism. Pragmatism.

Another problem comes into play here. Helen's idea is not only a new business – it's a new market. There really isn't anywhere in the UK that's a total single marketplace for all packaging-related activity. The closest competition is perhaps the Yellow Pages or the search engines. This presents both an exciting opportunity and a risk to investors – it's uncharted territory.

Available resources
Helen's life savings and her colleague Bryce are her only resources. After nine weeks of work, they've found their first knock-back. It's a blow, and they need not only fresh ideas, but also reassurance. They look for help to redevelop the plan.

The approach
Helen and Bryce approach an e-Commerce agency. They want to make sure the next shot they fire at investors hits the mark.

Choosing the model
The agency recommends a variant of the Market Portal model. There should be a two-phase approach, they advise. First, a small focused business that can generate good profits and make a good name for itself. This would be much narrower than the broad model that Helen had first thought of. Perhaps it would just focus on two slices of the Market Portal – two 'vortals' – materials and printing.

Second, they suggest that only after the first phase is successful should they widen the business idea to cover the entire market. The benefit of doing this would be not only to reduce the risk by starting small, but also to establish a secure foothold in the most visible niches of the market. This would allow Helen to build on her successes rather than juggle with too many balls at once.

Doing the research

The agency reworks Helen's original statistics. Helen and Bryce have a long track record in the print industry and are well connected to good information sources. The agency's new analysis throws up some interesting challenges:

- Most suppliers in packaging are struggling financially – the market is already highly competitive and highly price-sensitive
- Very few suppliers offer more than three services out of the proposed eight
- Big packaging buyers order different goods and services from different departments – in other words, there is little centralised buying
- Specialism is paramount – many buyers will go only to certain specialists for their specific procurement needs

The agency approaches several packaging companies to ask what their expectations would be of an online marketplace. Not surprisingly, the interest is in business development. But it's clear that the technology and sales skills of the vast majority of print companies are woefully inadequate. This is the major opportunity that the enterprise can exploit. Helen and Bryce use their contacts to research the price expectations and current processes of buyers.

Helen's research paints a healthy picture of demand. Steady growth is forecast: over a quarter of a million companies in the UK alone every year require packaging services of one kind or another. And, for the next two years, that number is forecast to grow by 2 per cent.

Segmenting the market

In Helen's original plan, she had proposed acting as an agent for suppliers. Her revenues would depend on how much she could sell on behalf of her suppliers. Now the agency suggests a more subtle approach, which depends on simple segmentation:

- Direct buyers – companies buying packaging services directly for themselves
- Commissioners – companies buying packaging on behalf of their clients
- Suppliers of packaging services
- Suppliers of print services

Each market segment can generate revenues for AllPack. The agency suggests a small membership fee for buyers and a modest commission fee for suppliers. That way, the price of trading is lowered for everyone.

But there are more ways to generate revenue from these market segments than by merely charging them for core services. Why not introduce a range of specialist services, tailored to the needs of each market segment? The agency suggests that Helen offer promotional and sales services to suppliers and tendering and advisory services to buyers. Together, they have created new revenue streams, using the segmentation above.

Selecting the right strategies

Next, they work on four groups of strategies – for the enterprise, for suppliers, for buyers and for competitors.

Business strategy

They choose 'automation strategy' for the new enterprise (*see* Chapter 6). This pushes high content and functionality to large audiences. It's appropriate for their complex offering, which requires a lot of time in configuring or choosing. A comprehensive site will be needed, which favours automated processes over human ones.

Supplier strategy

Helen and Bryce decide to recruit suppliers before customers. They'll offer high discounts for the first 500 to sign up, and they'll make it easy for them to register. This will mean careful creation of an appealing service to suppliers:

- sales services
- promotional services
- web brochure service
- catalogue service
- empathetic approach

The benefit of this approach is that they are loading 'product' into their market portal first. They can't open for business if there's nothing to sell!

Buyer strategy

The team discuss the approach to buyers. They decide to create a range of 'vortals' – vertical slices of their broad market portal.

- Materials (from cardboard to paper and sheeting to binding, etc.)
- Printing (on box, on pack, booklets, flyers, etc.)

- Forming (boxes, bags, crates, trays, etc.)
- Insulation (expanded polystyrene, beads, fillers, etc.)
- Graphics (design and typography services)
- Distribution (delivery and storage)
- Equipment (new and used equipment for sales or rent)
- Labour (specialists and staff available for hire)

They will introduce the vortals in two stages – materials and print first, and then the others in a sequence.

Competitive strategies

First-mover advantage applies well here. Although packaging services are an established market, brokering and pooling buyers and suppliers is a brand-new one. The agency suggests that Helen and Bryce prepare defensive strategies to combat competition from copycats and indirect competitors.

- Blocking attack: Becoming a one-stop shop, not just for buyers but also for sellers – by listening carefully to both groups and expanding the service range to block out competitors
- Niche defence: The creation of eight vortals will allow the site to specialise and be broad at the same time – the degree of specialism will help to combat the more general competitor

Setting targets

The team agree the two-phase approach. They set targets as follows:

Phase 1	Materials & print (2 vortals only)
Sales	£2m in year 1
Suppliers	1,000 companies signed up
Buyers	2,000 companies signed up

Phase 2	All 8 vortals
Sales	£4m in year 2
Suppliers	3,000 companies signed up
Buyers	6,000 companies signed up

Setting the budget

Now that the £2m sales target is agreed, the agency recommends a 10:1 revenue-to-cost ratio for the first year of trading. The total cost should be around £200k. They round it down to £160k to be safe, and draw up the following budget:

Item	Cost	Your Input
Commercial Planning		
Revenue Model Consultancy	£4,000	6 days
Brief Business Plan Consultancy	£2,500	3 days
Investor Preparation Consultancy	£2,500	5 days
Total	**£9,000**	
Architecture		
Structure & Page Maps Workshops & Design	£8,000	7 days
Functionality List Workshops & Design	£6,000	5 days
Total	**£14,000**	
Production		
Visual Design Fees	£7,500	4 days
Software Coding Fees	£125,000	Nil
Total	**£132,500**	
Implementation		
Hosting & Domain	£1,500	Nil
Software Licences	£3,000	Nil
Total	**£4,500**	
Grand Total	**£201,500**	
Maintenance		
Technical Support	£1,200 pm	Nil
Content Support	£1,000 pm	Half day pm
Total	**£2,200 pm**	

Creating people processes

Because they have chosen 'automation strategy', Helen and Bryce are deliberately looking to minimise people processes. However, they have several important customer processes that they cannot automate.

- Launch: Between the two entrepreneurs, they have an enormous number of potential buyer contacts (many are former customers), and long lists of known buyers. A telesales drive is favoured to launch the site.

- Supplier data loading: as more suppliers load their services, products and prices, more support is required for those with low skills. Helen and Bryce recognise the need for a human support service for data loading.

- Finance: the team set up a credit-checking and account-management process for handling supplier commissions. Although the payment process is automatic, they anticipate the need for managing phone calls, disputes and exceptional requests from suppliers.

The results

The site is built in eleven weeks and trading starts immediately. The first year results are below target but adequate:

Phase 1	Materials & print only
Sales	£1.7m in Year 1
Suppliers	1,400 companies signed up
Buyers	2,600 companies signed up

Their sales performance – although a little below target – was over ten times the cost of the website. The team know that the average spend per customer is lower than they had forecast in their revenue model. They readjust their Year 2 targets accordingly:

Phase 2	All 8 vortals
Sales	£3.5m in Year 2
Suppliers	3,000 companies signed up
Buyers	6,000 companies signed up

Recruitment agency, £75,000 budget

This case study is based on an enterprising individual taking the initiative herself and proposing to her seniors how the company should innovate profitably.

The enterprise

Company:	ExpertNow Ltd
Business activity:	Recruitment
Employees:	8
Turnover:	£1.0m
Serving:	B2B and B2C in UK markets
Key customers:	Large employers, small employers, employees
Years trading:	Start-up

The challenge

The big idea:	To build an alternative offering to the mainstream recruitment sites. The company would also like to create a sharp and alternative image which will drive their printed materials
The problem:	An overcrowded marketplace
Chosen site type:	Market portal (*see* Chapter 8)
Project manager:	Maxine, founder, currently running a department in an advertising agency

The starting point

Maxine works in the recruitment advertising department of a large ad agency. For some time, she's had an idea to start a new business from within the agency.

Her boss has been very supportive. He's asked her to prepare a three-page outline of her business idea and a summary of the benefits to the ad agency. Excitedly, Maxine has reviewed 25 recruitment websites and prepared an initial outline of the business plan.

She makes a pitch to three directors who have expressed interest in her idea.

Current market position
In her presentation, Maxine explains how overcrowded and competitive the online recruitment market has become. Prices are high, but falling. The big companies are swallowing the little ones. And differentiation between competitors has been dramatically reduced. There is a need – a gap in the market – for a much more personal service, one that is aimed at self-improvement, not merely job placement.

She sketches out a competitive market position, which would require higher-quality staff and better software than most:

	Self-improving	
	High	Low
High (Human)	*Us*	
Low		*Most competitors*

Competitors

Maxine outlines how inward-focused most competitors have become, instead of customer-focused. She demonstrates this by playing back ten taped phone enquiries she has made to the customer services departments of these competitors. The dialogues reveal:

- poor personal service and a lack of senior personnel
- a strong tendency to push her enquiry back online rather than take personal responsibility for helping customers
- absence of any web functionality or service that improves CVs, search skills, interview technique or personal development plan

In short, the opposite of what every candidate – or business – expects of a good recruitment company. She also revealed an average of 15 per cent growth among offline recruitment companies. This statistic, she argued, demonstrated the enduring demand for a high-quality, human recruitment service. What was needed, she proposed, was the perfect combination of superb service and superb website.

Available resources

Maxine concludes her pitch by asking for £100k and the commitment of two full-time staff to babysit the project.

The directors are impressed. They approve the project and pencil a £150k budget. They ask her to hire an e-Commerce consultant to steer the production of the site. They also attach to the project Archie, a manager from the creative team, for three months. The project is now a runner.

The approach

Building the team

Maxine appoints herself as chair and detective, Archie as the creative maverick and the consultant as the adviser and planner. She also invites an ex-colleague who is now an employer to sit in on the meetings to act as a client representative.

She gets everyone together for a kick-off meeting and sets a twelve-week deadline. She knows that she'll have to tie up launch PR closely to the production schedule, so the emphasis is going to be delivery on time.

Choosing the model

The consultant recommends a market portal model. They're working to a tight budget, so she also recommends a two-phase approach, the second phase being a 'bucket' into which they can pour any aspirations that they can't afford. There's bound to be quite a few.

She also recommends one key twist to the plot: filter out young and inexperienced candidates – specialise in experience. This will help to further differentiate the business.

Segmentation

The team agree the following key market segments:

- Candidates over forty years old, or with over ten years' experience in one industry
- Big businesses
- Small businesses

They aim to make money mainly from the demand side – from employers. But they also decide that they should charge a small fee to some candidates who might prefer to pay for self-improvement.

Selecting the right strategies

The consultant hosts a strategy workshop and they focus on the broad approach to the business and to competitors.

Business strategy

They all agree 'human strategy' (*see* Chapter 7) as an overarching business strategy. This is about delivering a convenient and effective website to underpin a large human operation. Customer focus will be achieved more by human service, less by technology.

Competitive strategies

They have identified from Maxine's research the two most dangerous competitors, known by their reputation for service. The team decide to attack using David v. Goliath strategies:

- Flanking attack: They will attack both competitors by striking at their weakest part – that of self-improvement. The ExpertNow site will have three key features aimed at improving candidates' success rate: a CV rewriter, a text-based interview improver and an online career guider.

■ Territorial defence – they will protect themselves from copycat reaction by overlaying a specialism in 'mature worker' candidates. This will be their territory. They will have to develop this segment quickly and then protect it.

■ Diplomatic nous – they aim to use good affiliate arrangements with professional bodies as their secret weapon. This will underpin their 'mature-worker' approach. The professional bodies have big memberships of management-level staff. They will have to devise services to help these organisations in order to secure their endorsement.

Setting targets

They decide on a very cautious approach to target setting. They know their project is ambitious, but in a competitive environment they should expect tough competition. They settle on an organic approach to growth, not investor-backed, nor needing multimillion-pound advertising. The team agree the following draft targets with the board:

☐ online sales from employers worth £650k by twelve months
☐ online sales from candidates worth £100k by twelve months
☐ 10,000 direct candidates by twelve months
☐ 5,000 referral candidates from affiliates by twelve months

Setting the budget

The team choose a conservative 10:1 ratio for revenue to investment. This means they have around £75k to play with. The consultant draws up a fee schedule:

Item	Cost	Your Input
Commercial Planning		
Revenue Model Consultancy	£3,500	4 days
Brief Business Plan Consultancy	£1,500	3 days
Investor Preparation Consultancy	£1,500	5 days
Total	**£6,500**	

Item	Cost	Your Input
Architecture		
Structure & Page Maps Workshops & Design	£4,000	3 days
Functionality List Workshops & Design	£2,500	1 day
Total	**£6,500**	
Production		
Visual Design Fees	£7,000	2 days
Software Coding Fees	£52,000	Nil
Total	**£59,000**	
Implementation		
Hosting & Domain	£1,500	Nil
Software Licences	£1,500	Nil
Total	**£3,000**	
Grand Total	**£75,000**	
Technical Support	£1,000 pm	Nil

Creating people processes

Finally, the team choose a simple approach to their human processes. They will take their own medicine and hire mature workers as consultants. They will use the site's database to produce a wide range of reports and statistics on site behaviour and user profiles. This will deepen their understanding of their employer clients and their candidate clients.

They will depend on the telephone and face-to-face meetings, not just the website. And they will encourage their senior staff to design their own processes. This will help to keep a human feel to the working culture, which should shine on the outside of the business and help to reinforce their position.

The site is designed and built in six weeks.

The results

The project is a measured success. Sales were a little lower than forecast because the prevailing market prices had declined between research and launch. But otherwise the site achieved its goals:

- online sales from employers worth £610k by twelve months
- online sales from candidates worth £80k by twelve months
- 12,000 direct candidates by 12 months
- 3,500 referral candidates from affiliates by twelve months

Overseas investment services, £145,000 budget

I've put this case study in as a gentle warning to Internet start-ups on what can go wrong. It's based on a real-life project that suffered at the hands of an entrepreneur who had a good idea and an unprofessional approach.

The enterprise

Company:	JJK Overseas Investment Ltd
Business activity:	Investment services, specialising in overseas biology investment opportunities
Employees:	15
Turnover:	£2.0m target first year
Serving:	B2B in UK markets
Key customers:	Large corporations, wealthy individuals
Years trading:	Start-up

The challenge

The big idea:	To launch a new investment fund for UK investors, specialising in bio markets and opportunities. The company would also like to introduce a high-profile information service to the UK's investor trade press and the financial sections of national online and print media
The problem:	No funds
Chosen site type:	Membership and shop hybrid (see Chapter 8)
Project manager:	Shelton, entrepreneur

The starting point

Shelton has been sitting on a brilliant business idea for six months. He's going to offer customers the chance to invest in a wide range of overseas biomedical businesses. He passionately believes in his source of good opportunities, Haltrack, a global biomed register, which is collated and published by a world-renowned information publisher. He has researched and produced his own business plan. His partner, Emilio, is an interior designer with strong views on design, and no knowledge of the biomed market.

Current market position and competitors

Shelton's research is good-quality. He understands his customers well, and knows the trends in biomed funding: they're towards smaller, more risky and more commercially focused investments. Many investors are returning to the biomed market after the late nineties bubble burst on genetically modified crops.

Unfortunately, Shelton hasn't much competitor information. What little info he has merely leads him to become more confident in his own high-quality, market-leading plan. All he needs, he says, is a big investor.

Available resources

He's hooked up with a good team of e-Commerce consultants, and he has just enough to pay them for the architecture and visual design of the site. He needs equity before he can fund the real build.

The approach

The project starts and the consultants agree with Shelton on a double-track project. They'll crack on with the architecture while he can focus on winning finance.

Commercial case

The consultants convene a series of workshops, in which it becomes clear that the business plan is inadequate, and that the revenue model is lacking considerably. The commercial case has not been thought through thoroughly. Shelton is reluctant to revise his finances. He also loses the interest of his first potential seedcorn investor (of four).

Recklessly, Shelton postpones the marketing planning workshop, and the competitor research, the strategy workshops and the market positioning. Instead, he wants to focus on the site – its design and build.

A major competitor launches its site in the UK with a flurry of press interest and city enthusiasm. The first-to-market slot has gone. Shelton agrees a 'second-place' strategy with the consultants, based on a 'superior-product' approach to marketing.

Design

Emilio wants a design and colour scheme that suits his personal taste. Shelton washes his hands of design issues – 'Emilio's in charge of visuals,' he says.

The designers duly deliver a look and feel that pleases Emilio but tests poorly among potential customers. The tests are conducted at the consultants' request and paid for by them to prove a point. Emilio is unmoved, and overrules any attempt to change his design ideas.

Business development

Meanwhile, Shelton has successfully signed up the online versions of three national newspapers and one bank as affiliates. He intends to 'white-label' the site to them – to republish key parts of his site on theirs, in their corporate colours. The deals he signs are lucrative, but depend on delivery within five months. Easily long enough, he figures, to secure funding and build the site. He also signs a contract with Haltrack to pay for access to their biomed opportunity feed. Haltrack cannot confirm delivery dates for their data feed. There is still no confirmed seedcorn investor.

Architecture

The site architecture workshops go well. After their completion, the two entrepreneurs ask for seven sets of revisions, mainly based on their gradual recognition that competitors and marketing must be addressed. Shelton still resists the consultants' requests for marketing and strategy workshops. This runs up costs and causes delays.

The consultants are starting to feel that the lights are on but there's no one home. There is a promise of major investment funding from a biomed enthusiast. The entrepreneurs commission the first phase of development, on the strength of this promise, much to the surprise of the consultants.

Work starts and proceeds well. After the first three weeks of coding, the Haltrack feed is not delivered. Coding work is held up. This is expensive for Shelton, who is paying daily for the feed. Now the consultants are worried. They halt production and ask for a project review. They agree to rerun the competitive positioning, marketing and strategic workshops. The major prospective seedcorn investor pulls out.

Now Shelton can't pay for work already completed. He also has an unfinished strategy, an incomplete business plan and debts.

The results

The consultants write off their bad debt. Shelton and Emilio fall out over money and the project is binned. Considerable personal wealth is wasted.

What would have prevented this? Planning. It was absent all the way through the early stages and it ultimately cost the entrepreneurs dearly.

Glossary

Architecture – the structure and blue-print of the website

Bandwidth – the amount of information that can be transferred down a line, usually measured in bits per second

Banner – a rectangular advert that appears on web pages

Click-through – the user clicking on an image or text link to 'click through' to another page or site

Domain name – the address of a website

e-Commerce – selling, transacting, or providing goods and services on the Internet

Extranet – a private part of a website which is usually given over to customers

Functionality – the action or things you can do on a web page or site, including the forms, the buttons, the commands issued by pages or executed by servers behind the scenes

Gateway – an interface into the database or raw content of a website

Hit – a download of a single item (page or image) from a website to a user

Intranet – a private part of a website which is usually given over to staff

Link – text or an image which when clicked loads a different web page or site

Page maps – a schema of a single page, which identifies the full content and functionality of each page

Plug-in – extra browser features which come as standard or can be downloaded from the Internet and 'plugged in'

Further reading

Allen, Kanya and Yaeckel, *Guide to One-to-One Web Marketing*, John Wiley & Sons, New York, 1998

Craven and Cumming, adapted from Ries and Trout, 'Immutable Laws of Marketing', 1999

de Kare-Silver, *E-Shock*, Macmillan Press, London, 1998

Dobbins and Pettman, *The Ultimate Entrepreneur's Book*, 1998

Downes and Mui, *Unleashing the Killer App*, Harvard Business School Press, USA, 1998

Godin, *Permission Marketing*, Simon & Schuster, New York, 1999

Handy, *Gods of Management*, Pan, London, 1978

Hoult, Wilson, Steers, Pollard, Jones and Green, 'Momentum Marketing', Incisive Research, London, 1998

Liberoff, *B2B e-Commerce Know-How*, Wired Sussex, London, 2000

Livine, Locke, Searls and Weinberger, *Cluetrain Manifesto*, Persus Publishing, London, 2000

Performance and Innovation Unit, 'e-commerce@its.best.uk', Cabinet Office, London, 1999

Postma, *The New Marketing Era*, McGraw-Hill, New York, 1998

Ridderstrale and Nordstrom, *Funky Business*, Bookhouse Publishing, Sweden, 2000

Schneider and Davis, 'Intranet Architecture', Web Zeit, New York, 2000

Seigal, *Futurize*, John Wiley & Sons, New York, 1999

Wilson and Gilligan, *Strategic Marketing Management*, Butterworth-Heinemann, London, 1997

Zeff and Aronson, *Advertising on the Internet*, John Wiley & Sons, New York, 1999

Index

WARWICK
BUSINESS SCHOOL

CENTRE FOR SMALL & MEDIUM SIZED ENTERPRISES

Warwick is one of a handful of European business schools that have won a truly global reputation. Its high standards of both teaching and research are regularly confirmed by independent ratings and assessments.

The Centre for Small & Medium Sized Enterprises (CSME) is one of the school's major research centres. We have been working with people starting a business, or already running one, since 1985. The Centre also helps established companies to reignite the entrepreneurial flame that is essential for any modern business.

We don't tell entrepreneurs what to do – just help them be more aware and better informed of the opportunities and pitfalls of running a growing small enterprise.

Much of our practical knowledge is gleaned from the experience of individuals who themselves have been there and done it. These kinds of business coaches rarely commit their observations to paper, but in this Virgin/Warwick series they have captured in print their passion and their knowledge. It's a new kind of business publishing that addresses the constantly evolving challenge of business today.

For more information about Warwick Business School (courses, owner networks and other support to entrepreneurs, managers and new enterprises), please contact:

Centre for Small & Medium Sized Enterprises
Warwick Business School
University of Warwick
Coventry CV4 7AL
UK
Tel: +44 (0) 2476 523741 (CSME); or 524306 (WBS)
Fax: +44 (0) 2476 523747 (CSME); or 523719 (WBS)
Email: enquiries@wbs.warwick.ac.uk
And visit the Virgin/CSME pages via:
www.wbs.warwick.ac.uk

Also available in the Virgin Business Guides series:

THE BEST-LAID BUSINESS PLANS
HOW TO WRITE THEM, HOW TO PITCH THEM

Paul Barrow

Planning is not just for start-ups – it's the key to successful business development and growth for every company, new or old. But once a business is up and running, it's all too easy to concentrate on day-to-day operations and work towards short-term goals. Even these should be assessed carefully. If you're launching new products and services, taking on more people, relocating to bigger premises, buying a business or selling one, you'll do it better if you plan it.

However, the all-purpose business plans advocated in most business schools aren't necessarily the best ones. You need a range of plans for different audiences and purposes. This book shows you how to present the right plan for the right audience – so you stand a better chance of getting what you need. The sound practical advice, case studies and exercises in this book will help you through the planning process and ensure that yours are indeed the best-laid plans.

ISBN 0 7535 0537 1

Also available in the Virgin Business Guides series:

KICK-START YOUR BUSINESS
100 DAYS TO A LEANER, FITTER ORGANISATION

Robert Craven

Too much to do, too little time? Feel your business could do with a tune-up, but are too busy running it to sort out the problems? With the fast, proven techniques in this book, you can transform your workplace into a powerhouse. You won't find textbook abstractions or irrelevant management school theories here – just dozens of practical ways to turbocharge any business.

The case studies, worksheets and practical exercises in the book will help you to take the pain out of business planning, increase your profitability and keep your customers. You'll find out how to identify your company's strengths and weaknesses and assess its potential, and learn the secret obsessions of all successful entrepreneurs.

ISBN 0 7535 0532 0

Forthcoming Virgin Business Guides:

DO SOMETHING DIFFERENT
PROVEN MARKETING TECHNIQUES TO TRANSFORM YOUR BUSINESS

Jurgen Wolff

IT'S NOT ABOUT SIZE
BIGGER BRANDS FOR YOUR BUSINESS

Paul Dickinson